THIS BOOK BELONGS TO
The Library of

....

....

Copyright @2023

All rights reserved. No part of this publication may be reproduced, stored in a retrieval system, or transmitted in any form or by any means, electronic, mechanical, photocopying, recording or otherwise, without the prior written permission of the Publisher.

Thank you for Purchasing my book and taking the time to read it from front to back. I am always grateful when a reader chooses my work and I hope you enjoyed it!

With the vast selection available online, I am touched that you chose to be purchasing my work and take valuable time out of your life to read it. My hope is that you feel you made the right decision.

I very much would like to know what you thought of the book. Please take the time to write an honest and informative review on Amazon.com. Your experience and opinions will be of great benefit to me and those readers looking to make an informed choice.

With much thanks.

Table of Contents

Spectrum Mandala Throw	27
Celtic Mandala Throw	40
Fall Comfort Throw	47
Tree of Life Afghan	51
Serenity Mandala Throw	64
Squared-Up Mandala	69
Starburst Mandala Throw	74
Cathedral Rose Window Afghan	82
Honey Bunch Blanket	95
Rainbow Star Baby Blanket	100
Alegria Afghan	104
Ellie Roo	111
Daystar Throw	117
Six-Pointed Star	121
Roundabout Throw	129
Stitch Guide	134
Metric Conversion Charts	141

SUMMARY

The Spiritual and Artistic Significance of Mandalas Crochet: Mandalas crochet holds a deep spiritual and artistic significance that transcends its physical form. Derived from the Sanskrit word for "circle," mandalas have been used for centuries as a tool for meditation and self-expression. The intricate patterns and symmetrical designs of mandalas crochet not only captivate the eye but also engage the mind and soul.

In the realm of spirituality, mandalas crochet is believed to represent the universe and the interconnectedness of all beings. The circular shape symbolizes wholeness and unity, reminding us of our inherent connection to the world around us. As we engage in the process of creating a mandala crochet, we are encouraged to focus our attention and intention, allowing us to enter a state of mindfulness and deep concentration. This meditative practice can bring about a sense of calm and inner peace, as we become fully present in the moment and let go of any external distractions.

Furthermore, the act of crocheting a mandala can be seen as a form of self-expression and personal exploration. Each stitch and color choice is a deliberate decision, reflecting the artist's unique perspective and creative vision. The repetitive nature of crocheting a mandala allows for a sense of rhythm and flow, enabling the artist to enter a state of creative trance. This process can be deeply therapeutic, providing a space for emotional release and self-reflection.

The artistic significance of mandalas crochet lies in its ability to blend traditional craftsmanship with contemporary design. While the origins of mandalas can be traced back to ancient cultures, the crochet technique adds a modern twist to this ancient art form. The use of yarn and crochet hooks allows for endless possibilities in terms of color, texture, and pattern. Artists can experiment with different stitches and techniques, creating unique and visually stunning mandalas that reflect their individual style.

Moreover, mandalas crochet has gained popularity in recent years as a form of art therapy. Many individuals have found solace and healing through the process of creating mandalas, using it as a means to cope with stress, anxiety, and trauma. The repetitive and rhythmic nature of crocheting a mandala can be soothing and comforting, providing a sense of control and stability in times of emotional turmoil.

In conclusion, mandalas crochet holds a profound spiritual and artistic significance. It serves as a powerful tool for meditation, self-expression, and personal growth.

Understanding Crochet Textures and Patterns of Mandalas Crochet: Crochet is a versatile and creative craft that allows individuals to create beautiful and intricate designs using yarn and a crochet hook. One popular crochet project that has gained significant attention in recent years is the creation of mandalas. Mandalas are circular designs that often feature intricate patterns and textures, making them visually appealing and captivating.

Understanding the textures and patterns of mandalas crochet is essential for anyone interested in creating these stunning pieces of art. The textures in mandalas can vary greatly, depending on the stitches and techniques used. Some common textures found in mandalas include raised stitches, popcorn stitches, and shell stitches. Raised stitches create a three-dimensional effect, adding depth and dimension to the design. Popcorn stitches, on the other hand, create small, raised bumps that add texture and interest to the overall pattern. Shell stitches, which consist of multiple stitches worked into the same stitch or space, create a scalloped or shell-like effect, adding a delicate and feminine touch to the mandala.

In addition to textures, mandalas also feature a wide variety of patterns. These patterns can range from simple and repetitive to complex and intricate. Some popular patterns found in mandalas include granny squares, starbursts, and floral motifs. Granny squares are a classic crochet pattern that consists of multiple small squares joined together to create a larger design. Starbursts, as the name suggests, feature a central point with radiating lines or stitches, creating a star-like effect. Floral motifs, on the other hand, often incorporate petals, leaves, and other botanical elements, resulting in a design that is reminiscent of a flower or plant.

To create mandalas crochet, it is important to have a solid understanding of both the textures and patterns involved. This can be achieved through practice, experimentation, and studying various crochet resources such as books, tutorials, and online forums. By familiarizing oneself with different stitches, techniques, and patterns, one can begin to develop their own unique style and create mandalas that are truly one-of-a-kind.

In conclusion, understanding the textures and patterns of mandalas crochet is crucial for anyone interested in creating these intricate and visually stunning designs. By exploring different stitches, techniques, and patterns, individuals can unleash their creativity and create mandalas that are both beautiful and unique. Whether you are a beginner or an experienced crocheter, the world of mandalas crochet offers endless possibilities for artistic expression and personal enjoyment.

Materials, Tools, and Color Selection of Mandalas Crochet: When it comes to creating Mandalas crochet, there are several factors to consider, including the materials, tools, and color selection. These elements play a crucial role in determining the final outcome and overall aesthetic appeal of the finished piece.

Firstly, let's discuss the materials required for Mandalas crochet. The choice of yarn is of utmost importance as it directly affects the texture, drape, and durability of the project. For Mandalas, it is recommended to use a medium-weight yarn, such as acrylic or cotton, as they provide the perfect balance between stitch definition and flexibility. The yarn should also be soft to the touch, ensuring comfort when the Mandalas are used as decorative items or even as functional pieces like coasters or table runners.

Moving on to the tools needed for Mandalas crochet, a crochet hook is the primary instrument. The size of the hook depends on the desired tension and the thickness of the yarn being used. Generally, a hook size between 3.5mm to 5mm works well for medium-weight yarn. Additionally, stitch markers are essential for keeping track of pattern repeats and maintaining symmetry in the design. A pair of scissors and a yarn needle are also necessary for weaving in loose ends and finishing touches.

Now, let's delve into the color selection for Mandalas crochet. The beauty of Mandalas lies in their intricate patterns and vibrant colors. When choosing colors, it is important to consider the overall theme or mood you want to convey. For a bright and cheerful look, opt for a combination of bold and contrasting colors. On the other hand, if you prefer a more subtle and calming effect, choose a palette of pastel shades or earthy tones.

To create a harmonious color scheme, you can follow a few guidelines. One approach is to select colors that are adjacent to each other on the color wheel, known as analogous colors. This creates a cohesive and soothing effect. Another option is to choose complementary colors, which are opposite each other on the color wheel. This creates a vibrant and eye-catching contrast. Additionally, you can experiment with different shades and tones of the same color to add depth and dimension to your Mandalas.

In conclusion, the materials, tools, and color selection are crucial aspects of creating Mandalas crochet. By carefully considering these factors, you can achieve stunning results and bring your Mandalas to life. So, gather your materials, select your tools, and let your creativity flow as you embark on this beautiful crochet journey.

Refreshing Crochet Skills of Mandalas Crochet: In order to refresh your crochet skills for creating mandalas, there are several steps you can take to ensure a successful and enjoyable experience. Mandalas are intricate and beautiful circular designs that can be created using various crochet techniques and stitches. Whether you are a beginner or have some experience with crochet, it is always beneficial to review and practice the basic skills before diving into more complex projects like mandalas.

Firstly, it is important to gather all the necessary materials for your crochet project. This includes selecting the appropriate yarn, crochet hooks, and any additional embellishments or accessories you may want to incorporate into your mandala design. Choosing the right yarn weight and texture is crucial for achieving the desired look and feel of your mandala. Additionally, having a variety of crochet hooks in different sizes will allow you to create different stitch patterns and adjust the tension of your work.

Once you have your materials ready, it is time to refresh your knowledge of basic crochet stitches. Start by practicing the foundation chain stitch, which is the starting point for most crochet projects. This stitch creates a row of interconnected loops that serve as the foundation for subsequent rows. It is important to maintain an even tension while working the foundation chain to ensure that your mandala does not become too tight or too loose.

Next, familiarize yourself with common crochet stitches such as single crochet, double crochet, and treble crochet. These stitches are the building blocks for creating various textures and patterns in your mandala. Practice working these stitches in rows and in the round to get comfortable with their execution and to ensure that your tension remains consistent throughout your work.

In addition to basic stitches, it is also helpful to review and practice special stitches that are commonly used in mandala crochet. These include popcorn stitches, picot stitches, and cluster stitches, among others. These stitches add dimension and visual interest to your mandala design, and mastering them will allow you to create more intricate and unique patterns.

Once you have refreshed your crochet skills and feel confident in your ability to execute various stitches, it is time to start working on your mandala. Begin by selecting a pattern or design that you would like to recreate. There are numerous resources available online, including websites, blogs, and social media platforms, where you can find free or paid patterns for mandalas. Alternatively, you can also create your own design by experimenting with different stitch combinations and color schemes.

Special Stitches Used in Mandala Throws of Mandalas Crochet: Mandalas are intricate and beautiful crochet designs that are often used to create stunning throws. These throws are not only functional but also serve as decorative pieces that can add a touch of elegance to any space. To achieve the intricate patterns and designs found in mandala throws, special stitches are often used.

One of the special stitches commonly used in mandala throws is the popcorn stitch. This stitch creates a raised, textured effect that adds depth and dimension to the design. To create a popcorn stitch, several stitches are worked into the same stitch or space, and then all of the loops are pulled through at once to create a cluster. This creates a small, puffy ball of yarn that stands out from the rest of the fabric.

Another special stitch used in mandala throws is the shell stitch. This stitch creates a scalloped edge that adds a delicate and feminine touch to the design. To create a shell stitch, a set number of stitches are worked into the same stitch or space, and then all of the loops are pulled through at once. This creates a fan-like shape that resembles a shell.

The cluster stitch is another special stitch commonly used in mandala throws. This stitch creates a dense and textured fabric that is perfect for adding warmth and coziness to the throw. To create a cluster stitch, several stitches are worked into the same stitch or space, and then all of the loops are pulled through at once. This creates a cluster of stitches that are worked together to create a solid and sturdy fabric.

In addition to these special stitches, mandala throws often incorporate other advanced crochet techniques such as color changes, post stitches, and intricate stitch patterns. These techniques allow for the creation of complex and visually stunning designs that are unique to each mandala throw.

Overall, the use of special stitches in mandala throws adds a level of intricacy and beauty that sets them apart from other crochet projects. Whether you are a beginner or an experienced crocheter, creating a mandala throw with these special stitches can be a rewarding and enjoyable project. So, grab your crochet hook and some colorful yarn, and get ready to create a masterpiece that will be cherished for years to come.

Reading and Interpreting Complex Patterns of Mandalas Crochet: Reading and interpreting complex patterns of mandalas crochet requires a combination of skill, patience, and attention to detail. Mandalas are intricate circular designs that are created using various crochet stitches and techniques. They often feature complex patterns and motifs, making them a challenging but rewarding project for crochet enthusiasts.

To begin reading a mandala crochet pattern, it is important to have a solid understanding of basic crochet stitches and techniques. This includes knowing how to create a foundation chain, single crochet, double crochet, and other common stitches. Familiarity with different crochet abbreviations and symbols is also essential, as they are often used in mandala patterns to indicate specific stitches or techniques.

Once you have a good grasp of the basics, you can start deciphering the pattern itself. Mandalas crochet patterns typically consist of written instructions, charts, or a combination of both. Written instructions provide step-by-step guidance on how to create each round of the mandala, while charts visually represent the pattern using symbols and colors.

When working with written instructions, it is important to carefully read and understand each line before proceeding. Pay attention to any special instructions or stitch variations that may be included. It can be helpful to read through the entire pattern before starting to get a sense of the overall structure and design.

Charts, on the other hand, provide a visual representation of the mandala pattern. Each symbol or color on the chart corresponds to a specific stitch or technique. It is important to refer to the chart key or legend to understand what each symbol represents. Take your time to study the chart and familiarize yourself with the pattern before starting to crochet.

As you begin crocheting the mandala, it is important to follow the pattern instructions carefully. Counting stitches and rounds accurately is crucial to ensure that the pattern turns out as intended. Markers can be used to keep track of the beginning of each round or any specific stitch placements.

In addition to following the pattern, it is also important to pay attention to tension and gauge. Tension refers to how tightly or loosely you crochet, while gauge refers to the number of stitches and rows per inch. Both tension and gauge can affect the size and overall appearance of the mandala. Adjusting your crochet hook size or yarn weight may be necessary to achieve the desired results.

Interpreting complex patterns of mandalas crochet can be a challenging but rewarding experience. It allows you to create beautiful and intricate designs using your crochet skills.

The History and Meaning Behind Mandalas Crochet: Mandalas crochet is a form of crochet that involves creating intricate and symmetrical circular patterns. The word "mandala" is derived from the Sanskrit language and means "circle" or "center." Mandalas have a rich history and hold deep spiritual and cultural significance in various traditions around the world.

The origins of mandalas can be traced back to ancient India, where they were used as a tool for meditation and spiritual practice. Mandalas were often created using colored sand, stones, or other materials, and were meticulously crafted to represent the universe and the interconnectedness of all things. They were believed to aid in the process of self-discovery and enlightenment.

Over time, mandalas spread to other parts of the world, including Tibet, where they became an integral part of Tibetan Buddhism. Tibetan monks would spend days or even weeks creating intricate mandalas out of colored sand, only to destroy them once they were completed. This act symbolized the impermanence of life and the importance of letting go of attachments.

In recent years, mandalas have gained popularity in the Western world as a form of art therapy and mindfulness practice. Crocheting mandalas has become a popular way for individuals to engage in a creative and meditative process. The repetitive nature of crochet stitches, combined with the circular patterns of mandalas, can be soothing and calming for the mind.

Creating a mandala crochet piece requires careful planning and attention to detail. Crocheters often start with a central motif and then work outward, adding layers of stitches and colors to create a symmetrical design. The possibilities for creativity are endless, as crocheters can experiment with different stitch patterns, color combinations, and yarn textures to achieve their desired effect.

Mandalas crochet can be used to create a wide range of items, including blankets, rugs, wall hangings, and even clothing. The finished pieces often showcase the beauty and complexity of the mandala design, making them visually stunning and captivating.

Beyond their aesthetic appeal, mandalas crochet can also hold personal meaning for individuals. Some people choose to crochet mandalas as a way to honor their spiritual beliefs or to connect with their cultural heritage. Others may find solace and comfort in the meditative process of creating a mandala, using it as a form of self-expression and self-care.

Incorporating Mandalas into Home Decor of Mandalas Crochet: Incorporating Mandalas into Home Decor is a wonderful way to add a touch of beauty, spirituality, and creativity to your living space. Mandalas, which are geometric patterns that represent the universe, have been used for centuries in various cultures as a form of meditation and spiritual practice. They are not only visually appealing but also hold deep symbolic meanings.

One popular way to incorporate Mandalas into home decor is through Mandalas Crochet. Crocheting Mandalas allows you to create intricate and mesmerizing patterns using yarn and a crochet hook. The process of crocheting Mandalas can be both relaxing and therapeutic, as you focus on each stitch and watch the pattern unfold.

There are countless ways to use crocheted Mandalas in your home decor. One option is to create a Mandala wall hanging. You can crochet a large Mandala and attach it to a wooden hoop or embroidery hoop, creating a stunning piece of art that can be hung on your wall. The Mandala's intricate design and vibrant colors will instantly draw attention and add a unique focal point to any room.

Another idea is to incorporate crocheted Mandalas into your throw pillows. You can crochet small Mandalas and sew them onto plain pillow covers, instantly transforming them into eye-catching and decorative pieces. The combination of soft yarn and the Mandala's intricate pattern will add a cozy and artistic touch to your living room or bedroom.

If you're feeling more adventurous, you can even crochet a Mandala rug. By using thicker yarn and a larger crochet hook, you can create a beautiful and functional rug that will not only add warmth to your space but also serve as a statement piece. The Mandala's circular shape will bring a sense of harmony and balance to your room, creating a serene and inviting atmosphere.

In addition to wall hangings, pillows, and rugs, you can also incorporate crocheted Mandalas into other home decor items such as table runners, curtains, and lampshades. The possibilities are endless, and you can let your creativity run wild as you experiment with different colors, sizes, and patterns.

Incorporating Mandalas into your home decor is not only a way to express your creativity but also a way to infuse your living space with positive energy and a sense of tranquility. The intricate patterns and vibrant colors of Mandalas have a calming effect on the mind and can help create a peaceful and harmonious environment.

Choosing Colors for Your Mandala Throws in Crochet: When it comes to choosing colors for your mandala throws in crochet, there are several factors to consider in order to create a visually appealing and harmonious design. The colors you select can greatly impact the overall look and feel of your crochet project, so it's important to take the time to carefully choose the right combination.

One of the first things to consider is the purpose or theme of your mandala throw. Are you creating it as a decorative piece for your home, or is it intended to be used as a cozy blanket? The purpose of your project can help guide your color choices. For example, if you're making a throw for your living room, you may want to select colors that complement your existing decor. On the other hand, if you're making a blanket for a child's room, you might opt for bright and playful colors.

Another factor to consider is the mood or atmosphere you want to create with your mandala throw. Colors have the power to evoke certain emotions and feelings, so think about the overall vibe you want to achieve. Warm colors like red, orange, and yellow can create a cozy and inviting atmosphere, while cool colors like blue and green can promote a sense of calm and relaxation. You can also experiment with different color combinations to create a specific mood, such as using complementary colors for a vibrant and energetic look, or analogous colors for a more harmonious and soothing effect.

Additionally, it's important to consider the color theory principles when choosing colors for your mandala throw. The color wheel can be a helpful tool in understanding how different colors relate to each other. Complementary colors, which are located opposite each other on the color wheel, can create a striking contrast when used together. Analogous colors, which are adjacent to each other on the color wheel, can create a more harmonious and cohesive look. By understanding these principles, you can create a visually pleasing color scheme for your mandala throw.

Furthermore, consider the yarn options available to you. Different yarn brands and types offer a wide range of color options, so take the time to explore different yarn collections and swatch different color combinations to see how they work together. You may also want to consider the texture and weight of the yarn, as this can also impact the overall look of your mandala throw.

Lastly, don't be afraid to get creative and experiment with different color combinations. Crochet is a versatile craft that allows for endless possibilities, so have fun with your color choices,…

Tips for Maintaining Even Tension in Rounds of Mandalas Crochet:
Maintaining even tension in rounds of mandalas crochet is crucial for achieving a polished and professional-looking finished product. Uneven tension can result in misshapen or distorted rounds, making the mandala appear uneven or lopsided. To help you maintain even tension throughout your crochet work, here are some tips to keep in mind:

1. Choose the right hook size: Using the correct hook size for your yarn is essential for maintaining even tension. If your hook is too small, your stitches may be tight and difficult to work with, leading to uneven tension. On the other hand, if your hook is too large, your stitches may be loose and floppy, resulting in an inconsistent tension. Refer to the yarn label or gauge swatch recommendations to determine the appropriate hook size for your project.

2. Relax your grip: Holding the crochet hook and yarn too tightly can cause tension in your hands and fingers, which can translate into uneven tension in your stitches. Try to relax your grip and hold the hook and yarn with a gentle and comfortable hold. This will allow the yarn to flow smoothly through your fingers, resulting in more consistent tension.

3. Practice consistent stitch size: Consistency in stitch size is key to maintaining even tension. Pay attention to the height and width of your stitches, ensuring that they are uniform throughout your work. If you notice any variations in stitch size, take the time to adjust your tension accordingly. This may involve loosening or tightening your grip on the yarn or adjusting the speed at which you work.

4. Use stitch markers: Stitch markers can be incredibly helpful in maintaining even tension, especially when working on complex mandala patterns with multiple rounds. Place a stitch marker at the

beginning of each round to mark the starting point. This will help you keep track of your stitches and ensure that you are working the correct number of stitches in each round, preventing any tension inconsistencies.

5. Take breaks and stretch: Crocheting for long periods without breaks can cause fatigue in your hands and fingers, leading to changes in tension. To avoid this, take regular breaks to rest and stretch your hands and fingers. This will help prevent tension build-up and allow you to maintain a more consistent grip and tension throughout your crochet work.

6. Practice, practice, practice: Maintaining even tension in crochet takes practice. The more you crochet, the more familiar you will become with your own tension and how to adjust it.

Mixing Textures and Techniques of Mandalas Crochet: When it comes to the art of crochet, one technique that has gained immense popularity is the creation of mandalas. Mandalas are intricate circular designs that are not only visually appealing but also hold deep spiritual and symbolic meanings. What makes mandalas even more fascinating is the ability to mix different textures and techniques to create unique and stunning pieces.

One of the key aspects of mixing textures in mandalas crochet is the choice of yarn. Different types of yarns have different textures, ranging from smooth and silky to chunky and textured. By combining yarns with contrasting textures, crocheters can add depth and dimension to their mandalas. For example, using a smooth and shiny yarn for the outer rounds of the mandala and switching to a chunky and textured yarn for the inner rounds can create a visually striking effect.

Another way to mix textures in mandalas crochet is by incorporating different stitches and techniques. Crocheters can experiment with a variety of stitches such as single crochet, double crochet, treble crochet, and even more complex stitches like popcorn or bobble stitches. By alternating between different stitches, crocheters can create interesting patterns and textures within the mandala. For instance, using a combination of single crochet and treble crochet stitches can create a raised and textured effect, adding visual interest to the mandala.

Furthermore, crocheters can also mix techniques such as overlay crochet or tapestry crochet to add even more texture to their mandalas. Overlay crochet involves crocheting additional layers on top of the base layer, creating a three-dimensional effect. This technique can be used to create raised motifs or intricate patterns within the mandala. On the other hand, tapestry crochet involves carrying multiple colors of yarn throughout the project, creating a woven-like texture. By combining these techniques with different stitches, crocheters can achieve truly unique and textured mandalas.

In addition to mixing textures and techniques, crocheters can also incorporate other elements such as beads, sequins, or embroidery to further enhance the visual appeal of their mandalas. Adding these embellishments can create a tactile experience and make the mandala truly stand out.

In conclusion, mixing textures and techniques in mandalas crochet allows for endless possibilities and creativity. By carefully choosing yarns with contrasting textures, experimenting with different stitches and techniques, and incorporating additional elements, crocheters can create stunning and unique mandalas that are not only visually captivating but also hold deep symbolic meanings.

Designing Your Own Mandala Throw of Crochet: Designing your own mandala throw of crochet can be a fun and creative project that allows you to express your personal style and add a unique touch to your home decor. Whether you are an experienced crocheter or a beginner, this guide will provide you with the necessary steps and tips to create a stunning mandala throw that you can be proud of.

To start, you will need to gather the materials for your project. This includes a crochet hook, yarn in various colors of your choice, and a pattern or design inspiration for your mandala throw. You can find a wide range of crochet patterns online or in books, or you can create your own design by sketching it out on paper.

Once you have your materials ready, it's time to choose the colors for your mandala throw. Consider the overall theme or color scheme of the room where you plan to display the throw, and select yarn colors that complement or contrast with the existing decor. You can opt for a monochromatic color scheme for a more subtle and elegant look, or go for a vibrant and eclectic mix of colors for a bold statement piece.

Next, you will need to decide on the size and shape of your mandala throw. This will depend on your personal preference and the intended use of the throw. If you want a smaller throw to use as a decorative accent on a couch or chair, a circular or square shape may be suitable. On the other hand, if you want a larger throw to use as a cozy blanket, you can opt for a rectangular or oval shape.

Once you have determined the size and shape, you can begin crocheting your mandala throw. Start by creating a foundation chain of the desired length, and then work the first row of stitches according to your chosen pattern or design. As you progress, you can experiment with different crochet stitches and techniques to add texture and visual interest to your throw.

As you work on your mandala throw, don't be afraid to make changes or modifications to the pattern or design. Crochet is a flexible and forgiving craft, and you can easily adjust the size, shape, or color scheme as you go along. This allows you to truly make the throw your own and incorporate your own creative ideas into the design.

Once you have completed crocheting your mandala throw, it's time to finish off the edges and weave in any loose ends.

Upscaling Throws to Bedspreads of Mandalas Crochet: Upscaling Throws to Bedspreads of Mandalas Crochet involves the process of transforming smaller crochet throws into larger bedspreads with intricate mandala designs. This process requires careful planning, attention to detail, and advanced crochet skills.

To begin, the first step is to select a suitable crochet throw pattern that features a mandala design. Mandalas are circular patterns that often incorporate various stitches, colors, and textures. It is important to choose a pattern that can be easily adapted and scaled up to fit the dimensions of a bedspread.

Once a suitable pattern is chosen, the next step is to determine the desired size of the bedspread. This involves measuring the dimensions of the bed and considering any additional length or width required for overhang or draping. It is important to take accurate measurements to ensure that the final bedspread fits perfectly on the bed.

With the measurements in hand, the next step is to calculate the number of stitches and rows needed to achieve the desired size. This involves some basic math skills and an understanding of crochet gauge. Crochet gauge refers to the number of stitches and rows per inch achieved with a specific yarn and hook size. By calculating the gauge of the original throw pattern and comparing it to the desired bedspread size, it is possible to determine the necessary adjustments to make.

Once the calculations are complete, it is time to gather the materials needed for the project. This includes selecting a suitable yarn in the desired colors and textures. It is important to choose a yarn that is durable and easy to care for, as bedspreads are often subjected to more wear and tear than throws. Additionally, a larger crochet hook may be needed to accommodate the increased stitch count.

With the materials gathered, the next step is to begin crocheting the bedspread. This involves following the original throw pattern, but making adjustments as necessary to accommodate the larger size. This may involve adding additional rounds or rows to increase the overall dimensions. It is important to pay close attention to the pattern instructions and make any necessary modifications to ensure that the mandala design is maintained and properly scaled.

As the bedspread takes shape, it is important to periodically check the dimensions and make any necessary adjustments. This may involve adding or subtracting stitches or rows to maintain the desired size. It is also important to periodically check the tension and gauge of the stitches to ensure consistency throughout the project.

Styling Tips for Throws in Home Decor of Mandalas Crochet: When it comes to styling throws in home decor, mandalas crochet can add a unique and eye-catching touch. Mandalas crochet is a technique that involves creating intricate and symmetrical patterns using yarn and a crochet hook. These patterns often resemble mandalas, which are spiritual and geometric symbols representing the universe in various cultures.

To effectively incorporate mandalas crochet throws into your home decor, there are a few styling tips to keep in mind. Firstly, consider the color scheme of your space. Mandalas crochet throws come in a wide range of colors, so choose one that complements the existing color palette of your room. If you have a neutral color scheme, a vibrant and colorful mandalas crochet throw can serve as a focal point and add a pop of color to the space. On the other hand, if your room already has bold and vibrant colors, a more subtle and neutral mandalas crochet throw can help balance the overall look.

In terms of placement, throws can be draped over various furniture pieces to create a cozy and inviting atmosphere. For example, you can drape a mandalas crochet throw over the back of a sofa or armchair to add texture and visual interest. Alternatively, you can fold the throw neatly and place it at the foot of your bed to add a touch of luxury and warmth.

Another styling tip is to consider the size and pattern of the mandalas crochet throw. Throws come in different sizes, so choose one that suits the scale of your furniture. A larger throw can be used to cover an entire sofa or bed, while a smaller throw can be used as an accent piece on a chair or ottoman. Additionally, pay attention to the pattern of the mandalas crochet throw. Opt for a pattern that complements the overall aesthetic of your space. For example, if your room has a bohemian or eclectic style, a mandalas crochet throw with intricate and detailed patterns can enhance the overall look.

Lastly, don't be afraid to mix and match different textures and materials. Combining a mandalas crochet throw with other textiles, such as faux fur or velvet pillows, can create a visually appealing and cozy look. Experiment with different combinations to find the perfect balance between comfort and style.

In conclusion, incorporating mandalas crochet throws into your home decor can add a unique and artistic touch. Consider the color scheme, placement, size, pattern, and texture when styling these throws.

SPECTRUM MANDALA THROW

Round upon round of gorgeous textures and colors come together to create this stunning throw that is sure to take center stage no matter where it is displayed.

① ② ③ ④ ⑤ ❻ **CHALLENGING**

FINISHED MEASUREMENT
54 inches in diameter

MATERIALS

- Universal Yarn Uptown Worsted medium (worsted) weight acrylic yarn (3½ oz/180 yds/100g per skein):
    3 skeins #333 purple iris (G)
    2 skeins each #314 lime (A), #306 pumpkin (C), #319 lavender (E), #325 cranberry (H), #305 peanut butter (J) and #323 steel grey (K)
    1 skein each #331 sapphire (B), #353 Donahue (D), #355 mint green (F) and #335 acorn (I)
- Sizes I/9/5.5mm and H/8/5mm crochet hooks or size needed to obtain gauge
- 1 stitch marker
- Tapestry needle

GAUGE
Rnds 1–4 in pattern with larger hook = 4 inches in diameter

PATTERN NOTES
Weave in ends as work progresses.

Join with slip stitch as indicated unless otherwise stated.

All rounds are worked with right side facing.

Chain-1 at beginning of round does not count as a stitch.

Chain-3 at beginning of round counts as first double crochet unless otherwise stated.

When starting a new round with a new color, place slip knot on hook and work first indicated stitch as normal.

SPECIAL STITCHES
4 treble cluster (4-tr cl): [Yo twice, insert hook in indicated st, yo, draw lp through, (yo, draw through 2 lps on hook) twice] 4 times, yo, draw lp through all 5 lps on hook.

3 double crochet cluster (3-dc cl): [Yo, insert hook in indicated st, yo, draw lp through, yo, draw through 2 lps on hook] 3 times, yo, draw lp through all 4 lps on hook.

Puff: Yo, insert hook in indicated st and draw up a lp, [yo, insert hook in same st and draw up a lp] twice, yo and draw through 7 lps on hook.

Shell: (2 dc, ch 1, 2 dc) in indicated st or sp. When working into a shell, work into the ch sp unless otherwise specified.

2 treble cluster (2-tr cl): [Yo twice, insert hook in indicated st, yo, draw lp through, (yo, draw through 2 lps on hook) twice] 2 times, yo, draw lp through all 3 lps on hook.

Treble crochet popcorn (tr-pc): Work 4 tr in indicated st, remove lp from hook, insert hook in top of first tr, pick up dropped lp and draw through st, ch 1 tightly to secure.

Single crochet popcorn (sc-pc): Work 4 sc in indicated st, remove lp from hook, insert hook in top of first sc, pick up dropped lp and draw through st, ch 1 tightly to secure.

THROW

With larger hook and A, ch 5, **join** *(see Pattern Notes)* in first ch to form ring.

Rnd 1 (RS): Ch 3 *(see Pattern Notes)*, 11 dc in ring, join in top of beg ch-3. Fasten off. *(12 dc)*

Rnd 2: With B *(see Pattern Notes)*, [2 **bpdc** *(see Stitch Guide)*, ch 1] around each dc around, join in first dc. Fasten off. *(24 bpdc, 12 ch-1 sps)*

Rnd 3: With C, [**4-tr cl** *(see Special Stitches)*, ch 4] in each ch-1 sp around, join in first cl. Fasten off. *(12 cls, 12 ch-4 sps)*

Rnd 4: With D, [**puff** *(see Special Stitches)* in next ch-4 sp, ch 2, **fpsc** *(see Stitch Guide)* around top post of next cl, ch 2] 12 times, join in first puff. Fasten off. *(12 puffs, 12 fpsc, 24 ch-2 sps)*

Rnd 5: With E, [**fpdc** *(see Stitch Guide)* around next fpsc, ch 2, fpdc around next puff, ch 2] 12 times, join in first fpdc. Fasten off. *(24 fpdc, 24 ch-2 sps)*

Rnd 6: With F, sk first ch-2 sp, [fpsc around post of next fpdc, working in front of ch-2 sp, dc in next ch-2 sp 2 rnds below, 3 dc in next fpdc, working in front of ch-2 sp dc in next ch-2 sp 2 rnds below] 12 times, join with G in first sc. Fasten off F. *(12 3-dc groups, 12 fpsc)*

Rnd 7: With G, **ch 1** *(see Pattern Notes)*, [fpdc around post of next fpsc, fpdc around post of next dc, dc in next dc, 3 dc in next dc, dc in next dc, fpdc around post of next dc] 12 times, join in first fpdc. *(36 fpdc, 60 dc)*

Rnd 8: Ch 1, [fpdc around each of next 2 fpdc, dc in next 2 dc, 3 dc in next dc, dc in next 2 dc, fpdc around next fpdc] 12 times, join in first fpdc. Fasten off. *(36 fpdc, 84 dc)*

Rnd 9: With A, sk first 2 fpdc, *bpsc around each of next 7 dc, bpsc around next fpdc, ch 15, **3-dc cl** *(see Special Stitches)* in 7th ch from hook, [ch 3, sk 3 chs, 3-dc cl in next ch] twice, sk next fpdc, bpsc around next fpdc, rep from * around, join in first bpsc. Fasten off *(see photo A). (12 petals, 108 bpsc)*

Rnd 10: With H, *sc in rnd 8 in center dc of first 3-dc group, sk next 4 sts on rnd 8, working along rnd 9 petal, fptr around bottom of first cl, [2 tr in next ch-3 sp, fptr around bottom of next cl] twice, 11 tr in ch-6 sp, fptr around top of next cl, [2 tr in next ch-3 sp, fptr around top of next cl] twice, sk next 4 sts on rnd 8, rep from * around, join in first sc. Fasten off *(see photo B). (12 sc, 12 25-tr petals)*

Photo B

Rnd 11: With I, *3-dc cl in next sc, sk next 3 tr, bphdc around each of next 19 tr, sk next 3 tr; rep from * around, join in first st. *(12 groups of 19 bphdc, 12 cls)*

Rnd 12: Ch 1, *fpsc around next cl, ch 2, sk next 3 hdc, sl st in next hdc, sc in next 3 hdc, ch 1, [sc in next hdc, ch 1] 5 times, sc in next 3 hdc, sl st in next hdc, ch 2, sk 3 hdc; rep from * around, join in first sc. Fasten off *(see photo C)*. *(12 groups of [11 sc, 2 sl sts, 2 ch-2 sps, 6 ch-1 sps])*

Rnd 13: With E, *4 tr-cl around next fpsc, sk next sl st and next sc, sl st in next sc, sc in next sc, ch 2, [sc in next ch-1 sp, ch 2] 6 times, sc in next sc, sl st in next sc; rep from * around, join with C in first cl. Fasten off E. *(12 groups of [1 tr-cl, 8 sc, 2 sl sts, 7 ch-2 sps])*

Rnd 14: Ch 1, *3 sc in cl, puff in next ch-2 sp, [ch 3, puff in next ch-2 sp] 6 times; rep from * around, join in first sc. Fasten off. *(12 groups of [7 puffs, 3 sc, 6 ch-3 sps])*

Rnd 15: With B, ***dc dec** (see Stitch Guide) in next 3 sc, sl st in next ch-3 sp, ch 1, **shell** *(see Special Stitches)* in each of next 4 ch-3 sps, ch 1, sl st in next ch-3 sp; rep from * around, join in first st. Fasten off. *(12 groups of [4 shells, 1 dc, 2 sl sts, 2 ch-1 sps])*

Rnd 16: With F, *sk next dc and sl st, sl st in next ch-1 sp, ch 1, shell in each of next 4 shells, ch 1, sl st in next ch-1 sp, ch 1; rep from * around, join in first sl st. Fasten off. *(12 groups of [4 shells, 2 sl sts, 3 ch-1 sps])*

Rnd 17: With J, starting at previous ch-1 sp, ***2-tr cl** *(see Special Stitches)* in ch-1 sp, sk next sl st and ch-1 sp, shell in each of next 4 shells, sk next ch-1 sp and sl st, rep from * around, join in first cl. Fasten off. *(12 groups of [4 shells, 1 cl])*

Rnd 18: With K, *[fpdc, 3 dc, fpdc] in next cl, shell in each of next 4 shells, rep from * around, join with D in first st. Fasten off K. *(12 groups of [4 shells, 3 fpdc, 2 dc])*

Rnd 19: Ch 1, *fpdc around fpdc, ch 1, [puff in next dc, ch 1] 3 times, fpdc around next fpdc, sk next 2 dc, working in dc and ch sps, sc in **back lps only** *(see Stitch Guide)* in next 16 sts, sk next 2 dc, rep from * around, join with G in first fpdc. Fasten off D. *(12 groups of [3 puffs, 2 fpdc, 16 sc, 4 ch-1 sps])*

Rnd 20: Ch 1, *fpdc around fpdc, ch 1, [puff in next ch-1 sp, ch 1] 4 times, fpdc around post of next fpdc, sk 2 sc, sc in back lps only in next 12 sc, sk 2 sc; rep from * around, join with E in first fpdc. Fasten off G *(see photo D)*. *(12 groups of [4 puffs, 2 fpdc, 12 sc, 5 ch-1 sps])*

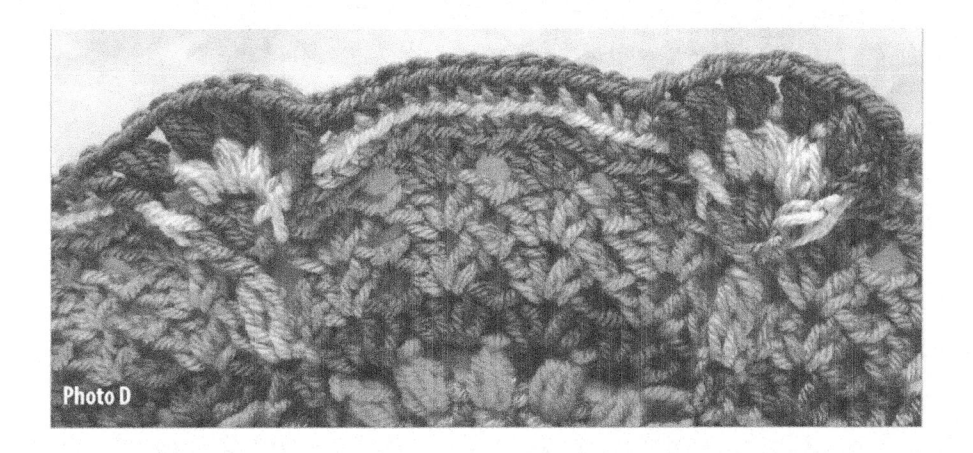

Photo D

Rnd 21: Ch 1, *fpdc around next fpdc, ch 1, 2 dc in next ch-1 sp, 3 dc in next 3 ch-1 sps, 2 dc in next ch-1 sp, ch 1, fpdc around post of next fpdc, sk next 2 sc, sc in back lps only in next 8 sc, sk next 2 sc; rep from * around, join with G in first fpdc. Fasten off E. *(12 groups of [2 fpdc, 13 dc, 8 sc, 2 ch-1 sps])*

Rnd 22: Ch 1, *bpdc around next fpdc, ch 1, bpdc around each of next 2 dc, ch 1, [bpdc around each of next 3 dc, ch 1] 3 times, bpdc around each of next 2 dc, ch 1, bpdc around post of next fpdc, sk 2 sc, sc in back lps only in next 4 sc, sk 2 sc; rep from * around, join with E in first dc. Fasten off G. *(12 groups of [15 bpdc, 4 sc, 6 ch-1 sps])*

Rnd 23: Ch 1, *bpdc around next bpdc, 2 bpdc around next 2 bpdc, [bpdc around next bpdc, 2 bpdc around next bpdc, bpdc around next bpdc] 3 times, 2 bpdc around next 2 bpdc, bpdc around next bpdc, sk next sc, sc in back lps only in next 2 sc, sk next sc; rep from * around, join in first dc. Fasten off. *(12 groups of [22 bpdc, 2 sc])*

Rnd 24: With A, starting in any 2-sc group, ***sc dec** *(see Stitch Guide)* in next 2 sc, ch 4, sk 3 dc, 3 sc in next dc, [ch 4, sk 4 dc, 3 sc in next dc] 3 times, ch 4, sk 3 dc; rep from * around, join with H in first sc. Fasten off A. *(12 groups of 13 sc, 5 ch-4 sps)*

Rnd 25: Ch 1, *sl st in next ch-4 sp, [ch 1, sk next sc, 7 dc in next sc, ch 1, sl st in next ch-4 sp] 4 times, sk next sc dec, rep from * around, join with D in first sl st. Fasten off H *(see photo E)*. *(12 groups of 28 dc, 5 sl sts, 8 ch-1 sps)*

Photo E

Rnd 26: Ch 1, *bpdc around post of next 3 dc, ch 1, bpdc around post of next dc, ch 1, bpdc around post of next 3 dc; rep from * around, join in first dc. Fasten off. *(48 groups of [7 bpdc, 2 ch-1 sps])*

Rnd 27: With J, sl st in center dc of first 7-dc shell of rnd 25, ch 4, sk (ch-1, dc, ch-1) on current rnd, dc dec in next 6 bpdc of current rnd, ch 4, *sl st in center dc of next 7-dc shell of rnd 25, ch 4, sk (ch-1, dc, ch-1) on current rnd, dc dec in next 6 bpdc of current rnd, ch 4; rep from * around, join in first sl st. *(48 groups of [1 dc, 1 sl st, 2 ch-4 sps])*

Rnd 28: Ch 1, *fpsc around next sl st, sk ch-4 sp, 9 tr in next dc, sk ch-4 sp; rep from * around, join in first fpsc. Fasten off *(see photo F)*. *(48 groups of [9 tr, 1 fpsc])*

Photo F

34

Rnd 29: With B, *[fpdc, ch 2, fpdc] around next sc, sk 2 dc, sc in next 5 dc, sk 2 dc; rep from * around, join in first dc. Fasten off. *(48 groups of [2 dc, 5 sc, 1 ch-2 sp])*

Rnd 30: With C, *[3-dc cl, ch 3, 3-dc cl] in next ch-2 sp, ch 2, sk next 2 sc, sc in next sc, ch 2, sk next 2 sc; rep from * around, join with D in first cl. Fasten off C *(see photo G). (48 groups [2 cls, 1 sc, 1 ch-3 sp, 2 ch-2 sps])*

Rnd 31: Ch 1, *3 dc in next ch-3 sp, 3 dc in next 2 ch-2 sps; rep from * around, join in first dc. *(48 groups of [3 3-dc groups])*

Rnd 32: Ch 1, sc in back lps only in each dc around, join in first sc. *(48 groups of 9 back lp sc)*

Rnd 33: With K, starting in first 3-dc group of a 9-dc group on rnd 31, *puff in center dc of 3-dc group, ch 1, sk next sc, [dc in next sc, fpdc around center dc of next 3-dc group 2 rnds below, dc in next sc on current rnd] twice, ch 1, sk 1 sc, rep from around, join in first st. Fasten off. *(48 groups [1 puff, 2 fpdc, 4 dc, 2 ch-1 sps])*

Rnd 34: With D, *puff in next puff, ch 1, dc in next dc, fpdc around next fpdc, dc in next 2 dc, fpdc around next fpdc, dc in next dc, ch 1; rep from * around, join in first puff. Fasten off.

Rnd 35: With K, rep rnd 34. Fasten off.

Rnd 36: With D, dc in each st and ch sp around, join in first dc. Fasten off. *(432 sts)*

Rnd 37: With B, tr in back lps only of each st around, join with C in first tr. Fasten off B.

Rnd 38: Ch 1, sc in next 5 tr, 3-dc cl in unworked front lp only of next st of rnd 36, sk next tr on current rnd, sc in next 5 tr, ch 4, **tr-pc** *(see Special Stitches)* in next tr, ch 4; rep from * around, join in first sc. Fasten off *(see photo H)*. *(36 groups of [1 tr-pc, 1 dc cl, 10 sc, 2 ch-4 sps])*

Rnd 39: With G, ***sc-pc** (see Special Stitches)* in next tr-pc, ch 1, sl st in next ch-4 sp, dc in 3 sc, sk 2 sc, 5 dc in next cl, sk 2 sc, dc in next 3 sc, sl st in ch-4 sp, ch 1; rep from * around, join in first pc. *(36 groups [11 dc, 1 pc, 2 sl sts, 2 ch-1 sps)*

Rnd 40: Ch 1, starting in previous ch-1 sp, work sc dec in next 2 ch-1 sps, place marker in sc dec just made, fpdc around each of next 11 dc, *sc dec in next 2 ch-1 sps, fpdc around each of next 11 dc; rep from * around, join with A in first sc. Fasten off G. *(36 groups of [11 dc, 1 sc])*

Rnd 41: Ch 1, *bpsc around next sc, bpsc around each of next 5 fpdc, ch 19, 3-dc cl in 7th ch from hook, [ch 3, sk 3 chs, 3-dc cl in next ch] 3 times, sk next fpdc, bpsc around each of next 5 fpdc; rep from * around, join with H in first sc. *(36 petals, 396 bpsc)*

Rnd 42: Ch 1, *sc in next sc, ch 1, sk next 5 sc, working along petal, [fptr around bottom of next cl, (2-tr cl, 1 tr) in next ch-3 sp] 3 times, fptr around bottom of next cl, 12 tr in ch-6 sp, fptr around top of next cl, [(1 tr, 2-tr cl) in next ch-3 sp, fptr around top of next cl] 3 times, ch 1, sk next 5 sc, rep from * around, join in first sc. Fasten off. *(36 groups of [6 cls, 26 tr, 1 sc, 2 ch-1 sps])*

Rnd 43: Change to smaller hook, with J, starting at marked st of rnd 40, work 3 tr in marked sc, *on current rnd, working in back lps only along next petal, sk next tr, sc in next 13 tr, 2 sc in next tr, sc in next 2 tr, 2 sc in next tr, sc in next 13 tr, sk next tr and ch-1 sp**, 3 tr in next sc from rnd 40; rep from * around, ending last rep at **, join in first tr. Fasten off *(see photo I)*. *(36 groups of [3 tr, 32 sc])*

Photo I

Rnd 44: With E, starting at first tr of a 3-tr group, *fptr around each of next 3 tr, sk 2 sc, sl st in next sc, [ch 2, sk 2 sc, 2 sc in back lps of next sc] 8 times, ch 2, sk 2 sc, sl st in next sc, sk 2 sc; rep from * around, join in first tr. *(36 groups [3 fptr, 16 sc, 2 sl sts, 9 ch-2 sps])*

Rnd 45: With G, sk first ch-2 sp after any 3 tr, *puff in next ch-2 sp, ch 2, 3 dc in next ch-2 sp, ch 2, 3 hdc in next ch-2 sp, ch 2, 3 sc in next ch-2 sp, ch 2, 3 hdc in next ch-2 sp, ch 2, 3 dc in next ch-2 sp, ch 2, puff in next ch-2 sp, ch 3, work dc dec in (next ch-2 sp, around front post of each of next 3 tr, and next ch-2 sp), ch 3; rep from * around, join in first puff. Fasten off. *(36 groups of [1 dc, 2 puffs, 6 dc, 6 hdc, 3 sc, 2 ch-3 sps, 6 ch-2 sps])*

Rnd 46: Change to larger hook, with A, starting in ch-2 sp before any 3-sc group, *[dc, ch 3, dc] in ch-2 sp, sk 1 sc, [dc, ch 3, dc] in next sc, sk next sc, [dc, ch 3, dc] in next ch-2 sp, [ch 4, sc in next ch-3 sp] twice, ch 2, tr dec in next 2 ch-3 sps, ch 2, [sc in next ch-2 sp, ch 4] twice; rep from around, join with C in first dc. Fasten off A *(see photo J)*. *(36 groups of [1 tr, 6 dc, 4 sc, 4 ch-4 sps, 3 ch-3 sps, 2 ch-2 sps])*

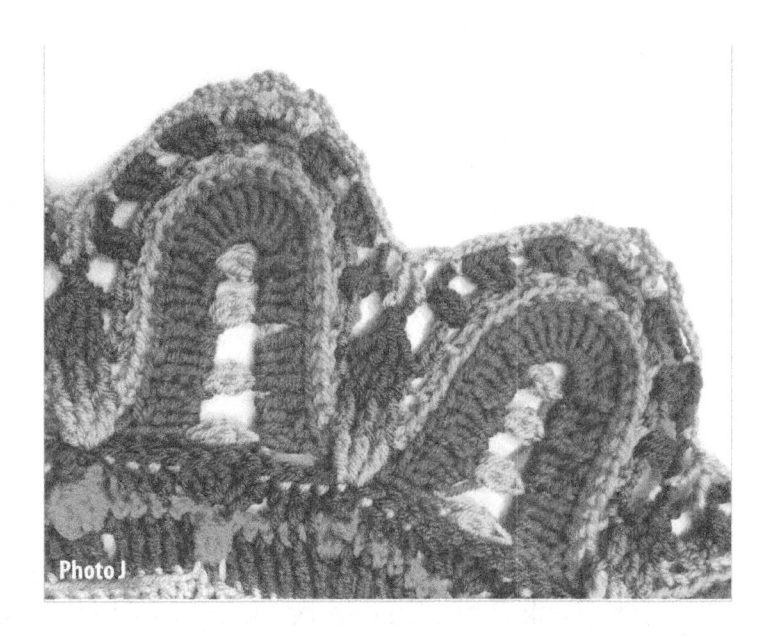

Rnd 47: Ch 1, *[3 sc in next ch-3 sp, ch 3] 3 times, [sc in next ch-4 sp, ch 1] twice, sc in next ch-2 sp, ch 1, sc in next ch-2 sp, [ch 1, sc in next ch-4 sp] twice, ch 3; rep from * around, join with G in first sc. Fasten off. *(36 groups of [15 sc, 4 ch-3 sps, 5 ch-1 sps])*

Rnd 48: Ch 3, 3 dc in next sc, dc in next sc, ch 3, *sl st in next ch-3 sp, [dc in next sc, 3 dc in next sc, dc in next sc, sl st in next ch-3 sp] twice, sk next 3 sc, (4 tr, ch 4, sl st around post of last worked tr, 3 tr) in next ch-1 sp, sk next 3 sc, sc in next ch-3 sp**, dc in next sc, 3 dc in next sc, dc in next sc, sl st in next ch-3 sp; rep from * around, ending last rep at **, join in top of first dc. Fasten off *(see photo K)*. *(36 groups of [7 tr, 15 dc, 1 ch-4 sp])*

FINISHING

Weave in ends. Block piece to measurements.

CELTIC MANDALA THROW

Bands of Celtic cables radiate from the center of this beautifully textured throw. Crocheting in a neutral color of worsted-weight yarn sets off the cables created by working crossed post stitches.

INTERMEDIATE

FINISHED MEASUREMENT

47 inches square

MATERIALS

- Premier Yarns Anti-Pilling Everyday Worsted medium (worsted) weight acrylic yarn (3½ oz/180 yds/100g per ball):
    15 balls #100-52 chinchilla
- Size I/9/5.5mm crochet hook or size needed to obtain gauge
- Tapestry needle

GAUGE

14 sc = 4 inches; 12 sc rows = 4 inches

PATTERN NOTES

Read instructions carefully as some rounds are not turned or joined in the standard manner at the end of the round.

Weave in loose ends as work progresses.

Join with slip stitch as indicated unless otherwise stated.

Chain-2 at beginning of round does not count as first half double crochet unless otherwise stated.

Each arrow stitch and elongated cable stitch counts as 4 stitches in total stitch count.

PATTERN STITCHES

Arrow St

Row 1 (RS): [Sk next 3 sts, tr in next st, working **behind** tr, dc in 3 sk sts] across.

Row 2 (WS): [Sk next 3 sts, tr in next st, working **in front of** tr, dc in 3 sk sts] across.

Cable St

Row 1: Ch 1, sc in first sc, [ch 3, sk next 2 sc, sc in next sc, turn, sc in each ch of ch-3 just made, sl st in next sc *(cable made)*, turn, working behind cable, sc in each of 2 sk sc] across.

Note: In next row, do not work in 3 sc of cables.

Row 2: With cables pushed to RS and working in sts worked in sk sts, [2 sc in next sc, sc in next sc *(3 sc behind each cable)*] across to last sc, sc in last st, turn.

SPECIAL STITCHES

Woven stitch (woven st): Yo, insert hook in indicated st, pull up a lp and draw through 1 lp on hook, yo, pull through both lps on hook *(first half completed)*, yo, insert hook in same st, pull up a lp and draw through both lps on hook *(2nd half completed)*.

Knurl stitch (knurl st): Work same as **reverse sc** *(see Stitch Guide)*.

Reverse slip stitch (reverse sl st): Insert hook in next st at right, yo, draw through lp on hook.

Front post Celtic weave stitch (fp Celtic weave st): Sk next 2 sts, fptr around next 2 sts, working in front of last 2 sts, fptr around 2 sk sts.

Back post Celtic weave stitch (bp Celtic weave st): Sk next 2 sts, bptr around next 2 sts, working in front of last 2 sts *(as seen from RS)*, bptr around 2 sk sts.

THROW

Ch 5, join to first ch to form a ring.

Rnd 1: Ch 2 *(see Pattern Notes)*, work 20 dc in ring, **join** *(see Pattern Notes)* to first st. *(20 sts)*

Rnd 2: Ch 2, (2 dc, ch 2, 2 dc) in same place as joining, dc in next 4 sts, [(2 dc, ch 2, 2 dc) in next st, dc in next 4 sts] around, join to first st. *(32 sts, 4 ch-2 sps)*

Rnd 3: Sl st in next st, [ch 2, 2 hdc] twice in next ch-2 sp, *[**fpdc** *(see Stitch Guide)* around next st, **bpdc** *(see Stitch Guide)* around next st] across to next ch-2 sp**, (2 hdc, ch 2, 2 hdc) in next ch-2 sp, rep from * around, ending last rep at **, join to first st. *(48 sts, 4 ch-2 sps)*

Rnds 4–6: Rep rnd 3. *(96 sts, 4 ch-2 sps)*

Rnd 7: Sl st in next st, (ch 1, sc, ch 2, sc) in first ch-2 sp, [sc in each st across to next ch-2 sp*, (sc, ch 2, sc) in next ch-2 sp] around, ending last rep at *. *(96 sts, 4 ch-2 sps)*

Rnd 8 (low front ridge rnd 1): Working in **front lps** *(see Stitch Guide)*, sl st in first st, sk all ch-2 sps and sl st in each st around, join to first sl st, **turn**. *(104 sts)*

Rnd 9 (low front ridge rnd 2): Ch 1, working in unworked **back lps** *(see Stitch Guide)* of rnd 7, [sc in each st across to next ch-2 sp of rnd 7, (sc, ch 2, sc) in next ch-2 sp] around, join to first sc, turn. *(112 sts, 4 ch-2 sps)*

Rnd 10 (arrow st rnd 1): Sl st in first st, (sl st, [ch 2, dc] twice) in first ch-2 sp, [work row 1 of **arrow st** *(see Pattern Stitches and Pattern Notes)* to next ch-2 sp*, (dc, ch 2, dc) in next ch-2 sp] around, ending last rep at *, join to first st, sl st in first ch-2 sp, turn. *[120 sts: 7 arrow sts between ch-2 sps]*

Rnd 11 (arrow st rnd 2): Ch 2, dc in first st, [work row 2 of arrow st to next ch-2 sp, dc in last st, (dc, ch 2, dc) in next ch-2 sp*, dc in next st] around, ending last rep at *, join to first st, turn. *(128 sts: 7 arrows, 4 dc between ch-2 sps)*

Rnd 12 (RS): Sl st in each st to first ch-2 sp, (sl st, ch 1, sc, ch 2, sc) in same sp, [sc in each st around to next ch-2 sp*, (sc, ch 2, sc) in next ch-2 sp] around, ending last rep at *, join to first st, **do not turn**. *(136 sts: 34 sts between ch-2 sps)*

Rnds 13 & 14: Rep rnds 8 and 9. *(144 sts: 36 sts between ch-2 sps)*

Rnd 15 (woven st rnd 1): Ch 1, sl st in next st, (sl st, hdc, ch 2, hdc) in first ch-2 sp, [**woven st** *(see Pattern Stitches)* across to next ch-2 sp*, (hdc, ch 2, hdc) in next ch-2 sp] around, ending last rep at *, join to first st, sl st in next ch-2 sp, turn. *(72 sts: 18 woven sts between ch-2 sps)*

Rnd 16 (woven st rnd 2): Ch 2, [hdc in next hdc, woven st in each sp between woven sts across, working last woven st in sp between last woven st and last hdc before next ch-2 sp, hdc in last hdc, (hdc, ch 2, hdc) in next ch-2 sp] around, join to first st, turn. *(80 sts: 18 woven sts, 2 hdc between ch-2 sps)*

Rnd 17 (woven st rnd 3): Ch 1, sl st in each st to first ch-2 sp, (sl st, [ch 2, hdc] twice) in first ch-2 sp, [sk next hdc, woven st in next st, woven st in each sp between woven sts across to last 2 hdc before next ch-2 sp, woven st in sp between last woven st and next hdc, sk next hdc, woven st in next hdc*, (hdc, ch 2, hdc) in next ch-2 sp] around, ending last rep at *, join to first st, sl st in each st to first ch-2 sp, sl st in first ch-2 sp, turn. *(80 sts: 20 woven sts between ch-2 sps)*

Rnds 18–25: [Rep rnds 16 and 17] 4 times. *(112 sts: 28 woven sts between ch-2 sps)*

Rnd 26: Ch 1, sc in first hdc, [2 sc in each sp between woven sts across, working last woven st in sp between last woven st and next hdc, sc in same hdc, (sc, ch 2, sc) in next ch-2 sp, sc in next hdc] around, join in first sc. *(240 sc, 4 ch-2 sps: 60 sc between sps)*

Rnds 27 & 28: Rep rnds 8 and 9 *(248 sts, 4 ch-2 sps: 62 sc between ch-2 sps)*

Rnd 29 (knurl st rnd 1): Ch 1, (sc, ch 2, sc) in first ch-2 sp, sc in each sc around, working (sc, ch 2, sc) in each ch-2 sp, join to first st, **do not turn**. *(256 sc, 4 ch-2 sps: 64 sc between ch-2 sps)*

Rnd 30 (knurl st rnd 2): Ch 1, working in front lp only, [**knurl st** *(see Special Stitches)* in each st across to next ch-2 sp, sk next ch-2 sp] around, join with **reverse sl st** *(see Special Stitches)* to first st of rnd, do not turn.

Rnd 31 (knurl st rnd 3): Ch 1, [(sc, ch 2, sc) in first ch-2 sp, sc in unworked back lp of each st to next ch-2 sp] around, working in both lps, join to first st, sl st in first ch-2 sp, **turn.** *(264 sts, 4 ch-2 sps: 66 sc between ch-2 sps)*

Rnd 32: Ch 1, [sc in each st around to next ch-2 sp, (sc, ch 2, sc) in next ch-2 sp] around, join to first st, turn. *(272 sts, 4 ch-2 sps: 68 sc between ch-2 sps)*

Rnds 33 & 34: Rep rnds 8 and 9. *(280 sts, 4 ch-2 sps: 70 sc between ch-2 sps)*

Rnd 35 (elongated cable rnd 1): With RS facing, ch 1, sl st in first st, (sl st, [ch 2, 2 hdc] twice) in first ch-2 sp, *[**fpdc** *(see Stitch Guide)* around next 3 sts, hdc in next st *(elongated cable st made—see Pattern Notes)*] across to last 2 sts before next ch-2 sp, fpdc around last 2 sts**, (2 hdc, ch 2, 2 hdc) in next ch-2 sp, rep from * around, ending last rep at **, join to first st, sl st in next st and in first ch-2 sp, turn. *(296 sts, 4 ch-2 sps: 74 sts on each side between ch-2 sps)*

Rnd 36 (elongated cable rnd 2): With WS facing, ch 2, {[hdc in next st, **bpdc** *(see Stitch Guide)* around next 3 sts *(elongated cable st made)*] across to last 2 hdc before next ch-2 sp, hdc in last 2 hdc, (hdc, ch 2, hdc) in next ch-2 sp} around, join to first st, sl st in each st to first ch-2 sp, turn. *(304 sts, 4 ch-2 sps: 76 sts between ch-2 sps)*

Rnd 37 (elongated cable rnd 3): Ch 1, (sl st, [ch 2, hdc] twice) in first ch-2 sp, {hdc in next 3 sts, [sk next 3 sts, hdc in next hdc, fptr around next 3 sts, working in front of last 4 sts, fptr around 3 sk sts *(elongated crossed cable made)*] across, hdc in last hdc before next ch-2 sp, (hdc, ch 2, hdc) in next ch-2 sp} around, join to first st, sl st in each st to first ch-2 sp, sl st in first ch-2 sp, turn. *(312 sts, 4 ch-2 sps: 78 sts between ch-2 sps)*

Rnd 38 (elongated cable rnd 4): Ch 2, {hdc in first 3 sts, [bpdc around next 3 sts, hdc in center sp between last st and next st of crossed cable, bpdc around next 3 sts, hdc in next hdc] across, hdc in next 4 sts, (hdc, ch 2, hdc) in next ch-2 sp} around, join to first st, turn. *(320 sts, 4 ch-2 sps: 80 sts between ch-2 sps)*

Rnd 39 (elongated cable rnd 5): Ch 1, (sl st, [ch 2, 2 hdc] twice) in first ch-2 sp, {hdc in next 5 sts, [fpdc around next 3 sts, hdc in next st] across to last 2 sts from next ch-2 sp, fpdc around last 2 sts] across, hdc in next 4 sts*, (2 hdc, ch 2, 2 hdc) in next ch-2 sp} around, ending last rep at *, join to first st, sl st in each st to first ch-2, sl st in ch-2 sp, turn. *(336 sts, 4 ch-2 sps: 84 sts between ch-2 sps)*

Rnd 40 (elongated cable rnd 6): Ch 2, {hdc in next 6 sts, [bpdc around next 3 sts, hdc in next hdc] across, hdc in each hdc to next ch-2 sp, (hdc, ch 2, hdc) in next ch-2 sp} around, join to first st, turn. *(344 sts, 4 ch-2 sps: 86 sts between ch-2 sps)*

Rnd 41 (elongated cable rnd 7): Rep rnd 39. *(360 sts, 4 ch-2 sps: 90 sts between ch-2 sps)*

Rnd 42 (elongated cable rnd 8): Rep rnd 40. *(368 sts, 4 ch-2 sps: 92 sts between ch-2 sps)*

Rnd 43 (elongated cable rnd 9): (Sl st, [ch 2, 2 hdc] twice) in first ch-2 sp, {hdc in next 3 sts, [sk next 3 sts, hdc in next hdc, fptr around next 3 sts, working in front of last 4 sts, fptr around 3 sk sts, hdc in next hdc *(elongated crossed cable made)*] across, hdc in each rem hdc*, (2 hdc, ch 2, 2 hdc) in next ch-2 sp} around, ending last rep at *, join to first st, sl st in each st to first ch-2 sp, turn. *(384 sts, 4 ch-2 sps: 96 sts between ch-2 sps)*

Rnds 44–46: Rep rnds 38–40. *(416 sts, 4 ch-2 sps: 104 sts between ch-2 sps)*

Rnd 47: Ch 1, sl st in each st to first ch-2 sp, (sl st, sc, ch 2, sc) in first ch-2 sp, sc in each st around, working (sc, ch 2, sc) in each ch-2 sp, join to first st, **do not turn**. *(424 sts, 4 ch-2 sps: 106 sts between ch-2 sps)*

Rnds 48 & 49: Rep rnds 8 and 9. *(432 sts, 4 ch-2 sps: 108 sts between ch-2 sps)*

Rnd 50 (cable rnd 1): Ch 1, sl st in each st to first ch-2 sp, (sl st, sc, ch 2, sc) in first ch-2 sp, [sc in next st, work **cable st row 1** *(see Pattern Stitches)* across to last st before next ch-2 sp, sc in last st*, (sc, ch 2, sc) in next ch-2 sp] around, ending last rep at *, join to first st, turn. *(35 cables, 4 sc between ch-2 sps)*

Rnd 51 (cable rnd 2): Ch 1, [sc in first 2 sts, work **cable st row 2** *(see Pattern Stitches)* across, to last 2 sts before next ch-2 sp, sc in last 2 sts, (sc, ch 2, sc) in next ch-2 sp] around, join to first st. *(442 sts, 4 ch-2 sps: 112 sts between ch-2 sps)*

Rnds 52 & 53: Rep rnds 8 and 9 *(456 sts, 4 ch-2 sps: 114 sts between ch-2 sps)*

Rnd 54: Ch 1, sl st in each st across to first ch-2 sp, (sl st, [ch 2, 2 dc] twice) in same sp, [sk next 3 sts, fptr around next 2 sts, working in front of last 2 sts, sk first sk st, fptr around 2 sk sts *(first fp Celtic weave st made)*, work **fp Celtic weave st** *(see Special Stitches)* across, sk last st before next ch-2 sp*, (2 dc, ch 2, 2 dc) in next ch-2 sp] around, ending last rep at *, join to first st, sl st in each st to first ch-2 sp, turn. *(464 sts, 4-ch-2 sps: 28 fp Celtic weave sts, 4 dc between ch-2 sps)*

Rnd 55: Ch 2, sk first 2 sts, bptr around next 2 sts, working in front of last 2 sts *(as seen from RS)*, bptr around 2 sk sts *(first bp Celtic weave st made)* [work **bp**

Celtic weave st *(see Special Stitches)* across to next ch-2 sp, (2 dc, ch 2, 2 dc) in ch-2 sp] around, join to first st, turn. *(480 sts, 4-ch-2 sps: 29 bp Celtic weave sts, 4 dc between ch-2 sps)*

Rnds 56–63: [Rep rnds 54 and 55] 4 times. **Do not turn** at end of rnd 63. *(680 sts, 4-ch-2 sps: 379 bp Celtic weave sts, 4 dc between ch-2 sps)*

Rnd 64 (border rnd): With WS facing, ch 1, *sc in sp between last dc made and next st, [sk next Celtic weave st, 9 tr in next sp between Celtic weave sts *(shell made)*, sc in next sp between Celtic weave sts] across to next corner, sk last sp between last Celtic weave st and first 2 sts of next corner, 12 tr in next ch-2 sp *(corner shell made)*, rep between [ ] across to next corner, sk last 2 dc, 12 tr in next ch-2 sp, sk next 2 dc**, rep from * to ** once, join to first st. Fasten off. *(76 shells, 4 corner shells: 18 shells between corner shells)*

FINISHING

Block as needed.

Tip

For additional instructions, watch these helpful videos by designer Bonnie Barker:

Video #1
Right-Hand Version: https://youtu.be/ljHXzxh3CH8 Left-Hand Version:

Video #2
Right-Hand Version: https://youtu.be/b6EcJNsCvXs Left-Hand Version: https://youtu.be/GYDdA80SiUI

FALL COMFORT THROW

This striking throw is created by alternating three self-striping yarns, which allows you to focus on the unique stitch pattern. Crocheted from the center out in Bavarian stitch, each new round of color adds to its visual complexity.

①②③④⑤⑥ **INTERMEDIATE**

FINISHED MEASUREMENTS
50 inches x 50 inches

MATERIALS

[3 LIGHT]

- Lion Brand Cupcake light (DK) weight acrylic yarn (5.3 oz/590 yds/150g per ball):
    2 balls #233 apple picking (A)
- Lion Brand Mandala light (DK) weight acrylic yarn (5.3 oz/590 yds/150g per ball):
    2 balls each #230 dragon (B) and #228 kelpie (C)
- Size H/8/5mm or size needed to obtain gauge
- Tapestry needle
- Stitch marker

GAUGE
Rnds 1-3 = 4 inches square

Gauge is not critical for this project.

PATTERN NOTES
Weave in ends as work progresses.

Throw is worked from the center out.

Every 2 rounds will change colors.

To get the desired effect for this throw, you will be changing colors every few rows by working from each ball. Let the colors fall as they are and do not cut the yarn.

Join with slip stitch as indicated unless otherwise stated.

Chain-4 at beginning of round counts as first treble crochet unless otherwise stated.

Chain-3 at beginning of round counts as first back post double crochet unless otherwise stated.

SPECIAL STITCHES
Cluster (cl): Holding back last lp of each st on hook, 5 tr in sp indicated, yo, pull through all lps on hook.

Back post treble crochet decrease (bptr dec): Holding back last lp of each st on hook, bptr around sts indicated, yo pull through all lps on hook.

Back post slip stitch (bpslst): Insert hook from back to front to back around post of st indicated, yo, pull lp through and through lp on hook.

THROW

Rnd 1: Beg with A, ch 8, **join** *(see Pattern Notes)* in first ch to form ring, [ch 4, **cl** *(see Special Stitches)* in ring, ch 4, sc in ring] 4 times. Do not join; work in continuous rnds. Mark beg of rnds. *(4 cls, 4 sc)*

Rnd 2: [12 tr in top of next cl, sc in next sc] around, join in beg tr. Fasten off. *(48 tr, 4 sc)*

Rnd 3: Join B in **back lp** *(see Stitch Guide)* in 9th tr of first 12-tr group *(corner made)*, **ch 4** *(see Pattern Notes)*, **bptr dec** *(see Special Stitches)* around same st as beg ch-4, each of next 3 tr, next sc and each of next 4 tr; ch 4, sl st in both lps at base of last bptr worked *(lower half of circle completed)*, ch 4, bptr dec around each of next 4 tr; ch 4, sl st in both lps at base of last bptr worked *(corner made)*, [ch 4, bptr dec around each of next 4 tr, next sc and each of next 4 tr; sl st in both lps at base of last bptr worked, ch 4, bptr dec around each of next 4 tr; ch 4, sl st in both lps at base of last bptr worked *(corner made)*] 3 times, join in 4th ch of beg ch-4. *(4 lower half circles, 4 corners)*

Rnd 4: [8 tr in top of bptr dec, sc in next sl st, 12 tr in top of next corner, sc in next sl st] around, join in beg tr. Fasten off.

Rnd 5: Join C in back lp of 9th tr of any 12-tr corner, ch 4, bptr dec around same st as beg ch-4, each of next 3 tr, next sc and each of next 4 tr; ch 4, sl st in both lps at base of last bptr worked, ch 4, bptr dec around each of next 4 tr, next sc and each of next 4 tr; ch 4, sl st in both lps at base of last bptr worked, ch 4, bptr dec around each of next 4 tr; ch 4, sl st in both lps at base of last bptr worked, * [ch 4, bptr dec around each of next 4 tr, next sc and each of next 4 tr; ch 4, sl st in both lps at base of last bptr worked] twice, ch 4, bptr dec around each of next 4 tr; ch 4, sl st in both lps at base of last bptr worked, rep from * around, join in 4th ch of beg ch-4. *(80 tr, 8 sc)*

Rnd 6: *[8 tr in center of bptr dec, sc in next sl st] across to next corner, 12 tr in center of corner, sc in next sl st, rep from * around, join in beg tr. Fasten off.

Continue in this manner to work 2 rnds of A, 2 rnds of B and 2 rnds of C. Work in this sequence until Throw measures 50 inches square. At end of last rnd, fasten off.

Border

Rnd 1: With color of your choosing, **bpslst** *(see Special Stitches)* around first tr of any corner circle, **ch 3** *(see Pattern Notes)*, bpdc around next tr, **bphdc** *(see Stitch Guide)* around each of next 2 tr, **bpsc** *(see Stitch Guide)* around each of next 2 tr, ch 3, bpsc around each of next 2 tr, bphdc around each of next 2 tr, bpdc around each of next 2 tr, *bptr around next sc, bpdc around next tr, bphdc around next tr, bpsc around each of next 4 tr, bphdc around next tr, bpdc around next tr, rep from * across to next corner, [bpdc around each of next 2 tr, bphdc around each of next 2 tr, bpsc around each of next 2 tr, ch 3, bpsc around each of next 2 tr, bphdc around each of next 2 tr, bpdc around each of next 2 tr] rep from * for rem sides, join in 3rd ch of beg ch-3. Fasten off.

Rnds 2 & 3: With color of your choosing, *3 sc in any corner, sc in each st around, rep from * for rem 3 sides, join in first sc. Fasten off.

Rnd 4: Join any color in any st, working from left to right, **reverse sc** *(see Stitch Guide)* in each st around, join in first st. Fasten off.

TREE OF LIFE AFGHAN

The mighty oak tree was the inspiration for this stunning fall-themed afghan. At the center, a cross-section of the tree is surrounded by rounds of acorns and fall foliage. The photos detail many of the techniques used to create this one-of-a-kind project.

①②③**④**⑤⑥ **INTERMEDIATE**

FINISHED MEASUREMENT
54 inches square

MATERIALS

- Plymouth Yarn Encore Worsted medium (worsted) weight acrylic/wool yarn (3½ oz/200 yds/100g per ball):
    5 balls #1445 burnished heather
    3 balls #1415 fawn mix
    2 balls each #0212 cinnabar, #0456 harvest, #1233 greenhouse and #0462 woodbine
- Size H/8/5mm crochet hook or size needed to obtain gauge
- Tapestry needle

GAUGE
Rnds 1–3 = 4½ inches across

PATTERN NOTES
All rounds are worked with right side facing unless otherwise stated.

Weave in loose ends as work progresses.

Join with slip stitch as indicated unless otherwise stated.

Chain-4 at beginning of round counts as first treble crochet unless otherwise stated.

Chain-3 at beginning of round counts as first double crochet unless otherwise stated.

Chain-2 at beginning of round counts as first double crochet unless otherwise stated.

SPECIAL STITCHES
Cable decrease stitch (cable dec st): Keeping last lp of each st on hook, fptr around next st, dc in each of next 2 dc, fptr around next st, yo and draw through all 5 lps on hook.

3-double treble crochet cluster (3-dtr cl): Yo 3 times, insert hook in indicated st, yo, pull up a lp, [yo, draw through 2 lps on hook] 3 times, *yo 3 times, insert hook in same st, yo, draw up a lp, [yo, draw through 2 lps on hook] 3 times, rep from * once, yo, draw through all 4 lps on hook.

2-double treble crochet cluster (2-dtr cl): Yo 3 times, insert hook in indicated st, draw up a lp, [yo, draw through 2 lps on hook] 3 times, yo 3 times, insert hook in same st, draw up a lp, [yo, draw through 2 lps on hook] 3 times, yo, draw through all 3 lps on hook.

Single crochet join (sc join): Place slip knot on hook, insert hook in indicated st, yo and pull up a lp, yo and draw through both lps on hook.

Beginning 3-double crochet cluster (beg 3-dc cl): Ch 1, sl st in next sc, ch 2, [yo, insert hook in same st, yo, pull up a lp, yo, draw through 2 lps on hook] twice, yo and draw through all 3 lps on hook.

3-double crochet cluster (3-dc cl): Yo, insert hook in indicated st, pull up a lp, yo, draw through 2 lps on hook, [yo, insert hook in same st, yo, pull up a lp, yo, draw through 2 lps] twice, yo, draw through all 4 lps on hook.

Left Cross cable (LC cable): Sk next st, dc in each of next 2 sts, inserting hook from back to front, tr in sk st.

Right Cross cable (RC cable): Sk next 2 dc, tr in next tr, working behind st just made, dc in first sk st, dc in 2nd sk st.

AFGHAN

Rnd 1: With fawn mix, ch 5, 15 tr in 5th ch from hook *(beg sk chs count as first tr)*, **join** *(see Pattern Notes)* in top of beg ch. *(16 tr)*

Rnd 2: Ch 4 *(see Pattern Notes)*, tr in same st as join, 2 tr in each st around, join in top of beg ch-4. *(32 tr)*

Rnd 3: Ch 3 *(see Pattern Notes)*, 2 dc in same st as join, * **fptr** *(see Stitch Guide)* around next st**, 3 dc in next st, rep from * around, ending last rep at **, join in top of beg ch-3. *(16 fptr, 48 dc)*

Rnd 4: Ch 3, *2 dc in next st, dc in next st, fptr around next st**, dc in next st, rep from * around, ending last rep at **, join in top of beg ch-3. *(16 fptr, 64 dc)*

Rnd 5: Sl st in next dc, ch 3, dc in next dc, *sk next dc, fptr around next fptr *(Photo 1)*, working behind fptr, dc in sk st *(Photo 2)*, dc in next dc *(Photo 3)*, working in front of last st, fptr again around previously worked fptr** *(Photo 4)*, dc in each of next 2 dc, rep from * around, ending last rep at **, join in top of beg ch 3. *(32 fptr, 64 dc)*

Rnd 6: Ch 2 *(see Pattern Notes)*, keeping last lp of each st on hook, dc in next dc, fptr around next fptr *(Photo 5)*, yo and draw through all 3 lps on hook *(Photo 6)*, *2 dc in each of next 2 dc**, **cable dec st** *(see Special Stitches and Photos 7*

and 8), rep from * around, ending last rep at **, yo twice, insert hook from front to back around last fptr, yo and draw lp through, [yo, draw through 2 lps on hook] twice, insert hook from front to back around first fptr *(Photo 9)*, yo and draw lp through fptr and through both lps on hook *(join made; Photo 10)*. *(16 dec sts, 64 dc)*

Photo 5

Photo 6

Photo 7

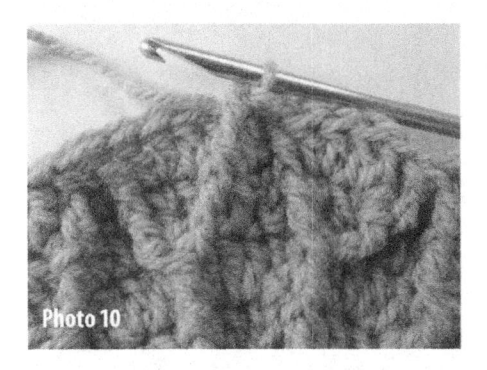

Rnd 7: Ch 4, dtr in same st as join, *(beg 2-dtr cl made)* (ch 3, **3-dtr cl**—*see Special Stitches*, ch 3, **2-dtr cl**—*see Special Stitches*) in same st *(first corner made; Photo 11)*, *sk next dc, tr in each of next 2 sts, dc in each of next 3 sts, hdc in each of next 2 sts, sc in each of next 3 sts, hdc in each of next 2 sts, dc in each of next 3 sts, tr in each of next 2 sts, sk next st**, (2-dtr cl, ch 3, 3-dtr cl, ch 3, 2-dtr cl) in next st *(corner made)*, rep from * around, ending last rep at **, join in top of beg 2-dtr cl, fasten off. *(68 sts, 4 corners; 17 sts between corners)*

Photo 11

Rnd 8: With RS facing, **sc join** *(see Special Stitches)* burnished heather in top of any 3-dtr cl, (ch 1, sc) in same st, *3 sc in next sp, sc in next cl, *sc in each of next 17 sts, sc in next cl, 3 sc in next sp**, (sc, ch 1, sc) in next cl, rep from * around, ending last rep at **, join in beg sc, **turn**. *(108 sc, 4 ch-1 corners; 27 sc between corners)*

Rnd 9 (WS): **Beg 3-dc cl** *(see Special Stitches and Photo 12)*, *[ch 1, sk next sc, **3-dc cl** *(see Special Stitches)* in next sc] around to next corner, ch 1, sk next sc, (2 dc, ch 1, 2 dc) in ch-1 corner sp**, rep from * around, ending last rep at **, ch 1, sk next sc, join in top of beg cl, turn. *(52 cls, 16 dc, 56 ch-1 sps, 4 ch-1 corner sps; 13 cls, 4 dc, 14 ch-1 sps between ch-1 corners)*

Photo 12

Rnd 10: Ch 1, sc in same st as join, *sc in next ch-1 sp, sc in each of next 2 dc, (sc, ch 1, sc) in next ch-1 corner sp, sc in each of next 2 dc, [sc in next ch-1 sp**, sc in next cl] around to next corner, rep from * around, ending last rep at **, join in beg sc, fasten off. *(132 sc, 4 ch-1 corner sps; 33 sc between ch-1 corners)*

Rnd 11: With RS facing, join cinnabar in any ch-1 corner sp, ch 4, 4 tr in same sp *(first corner made; Photo 13)*, *[tr in each of next 3 sc, dc in next sc, hdc in next sc, sc in each of next 3 sc, hdc in next sc, dc in next sc] around to next corner, tr in each of next 3 sc**, 5 tr in next ch-1 corner sp *(corner made)*, rep from * around, ending last rep at **, join in top of beg ch-4, fasten off. *(132 sts, 4 5-tr corners; 33 sts between corners)*

Photo 13

Rnd 12: With RS facing, sc join harvest in center tr of any 5-tr corner *(Photo 14)*, 2 sc in same st *(corner made)*, *sc in each of next 5 tr, [hdc in next dc, dc in next hdc, tr in each of next 3 sc, dc in next hdc, hdc in next dc, sc in each of next 3 tr] around to next corner, sc in each of next 2 tr**, 3 sc in next tr *(corner made)*, rep from * around, ending last rep at **, join in beg sc. *(148 sc, 4 3-sc corners; 37 sts between corners)*

Photo 14

Rnd 13: Ch 1, sc in same st as join, *3 sc in corner st, sc in each of next 6 sc, [hdc in next hdc, dc in next dc, tr in each of next 3 tr, dc in next dc, hdc in next hdc, sc in each of next 3 sc] around to next corner**, sc in each of next 3 sc, rep from * around, ending last rep at **, sc in next st, join in beg sc, fasten off *(Photo 15)*. *(156 sts, 4 3-sc corners; 39 sts between corners)*

Photo 15

Rnd 14: Join cinnabar in 2nd sc of any 3-sc corner, ch 4, 4 tr in same st, *tr in each of next 7 sc, [dc in next hdc, hdc in next dc, sc in each of next 3 tr, hdc in next dc, dc in next hdc, tr in each of next 3 sc] around to last 4 sc before center st of next corner, tr in each of next 4 sc**, 5 tr in corner sc, rep from * around, ending last rep at **, join in top of beg ch-4, fasten off *(Photo 15)*. *(164 sts, 4 5-tr corners; 41 sts between corners)*

Rnd 15: With RS facing, sc join burnished heather in 3rd tr of any 5-tr corner, (ch 1, sc) in same st as join, sc in each st to 3rd tr of next corner**, (sc, ch 1, sc) in 3rd tr, rep from * around, ending last rep at **, join, **turn**. *(188 sts, 4 ch-1 corner sps; 47 sc between ch-1 sps)*

Rnds 16 (WS) & 17: Rep rnds 9 and 10. *(212 sc, 4 ch-1 corner sps; 53 sc between ch-1 sps)*

Rnd 18: With harvest, rep rnd 11. *(212 sts; 4 5-tr corners; 53 sts between corners)*

Rnds 19 & 20: With cinnabar, rep rnds 12 and 13. *(236 sts, 4 3-sc corners; 59 sts between corners)*

Rnd 21: With harvest, rep rnd 14. *(244 sts, 4 5-tr corners; 61 sts between corners)*

Rnd 22: Rep rnd 15. *(268 sts, 4 ch-1 corner sps; 67 sc between ch-1 sps)*

Rnds 23–29: Rep rnds 9–15. *(348 sts, 4 ch-1 corner sps, 87 sc between ch-1 sps)*

Rnds 30 & 31: Rep rnds 9 and 10. *(372 sts, 4 ch-1 corner sps; 93 sts between ch-1 sps)*

Rnd 32: With RS facing, sc join fawn mix in any ch-1 corner sp, 2 sc in same sp, sc in each st around, working 3 sc in each ch-1 sp, join in beg sc. *(372 sts, 4 3-sc corners; 93 sts between corners)*

Rnd 33: Ch 3, *(2 dc, ch 1, 2 dc) in next st *(center st of 3-sc corner)*, dc in next sc, [**LC cable** *(see Special Stitches and Photos 16–18)* in next 3 sts] around to next 3-sc corner**, dc in next sc, rep from * around, ending last rep at **, join. *(124 LC cables, 24 dc, 4 ch-1 corner sps; 31 LC cables, 6 dc between ch-1 sps)*

Photo 16

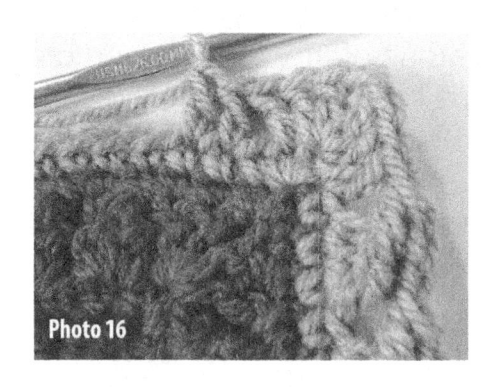

Photo 17

Photo 18

Rnd 34: Ch 3, dc in each of next 2 dc, *(2 dc, ch 1, 2 dc) in ch-1 corner sp, dc in each of next 3 dc, [**RC cable** *(see Special Stitches and Photos 19–21)* in next 3 sts] around to last 3 sts before next corner ch-1 sp**, dc in each of next 3 dc, rep from * around, ending last rep at **, join in top of beg ch-3. *(124 RC cables, 40 dc, 4 ch-1 corner sps; 31 RC cables, 10 dc between ch-1 sps)*

Rnd 35: Ch 1, sc in same st as join, *sc in each st to next corner**, 3 sc in corner ch-1 sp, rep from * around, ending last rep at **, join in beg sc, fasten off. *(412 sts, 4 3-sc corners; 103 sc between corners)*

Rnd 36: With RS facing, sc join burnished heather in 2nd sc of any 3-sc corner, (ch 1, sc) in same st, sc in each st around, working (sc, ch 1, sc) in 2nd sc of each 3-sc corner, join in beg sc, turn. *(428 sts, 4 ch-1 corner sps; 107 sc between ch-1 sps)*

Rnds 37 & 38: Reps rnd 9 and 10. *(452 sts, 4 ch-1 corner sps; 113 sc between ch-1 sps)*

Rnd 39: With greenhouse, rep rnd 11. *(452 sts, 4 5-tr corners; 113 sts between corners)*

Rnds 40 & 41: With woodbine, rep rnds 12 and 13. *(476 sts, 4 3-sc corners; 119 sts between corners)*

Rnd 42: With greenhouse, rep rnd 14. *(484 sts, 4 5-tr corners; 121 sts between corners)*

Rnd 43: Rep rnd 15. *(508 sts, 4 ch-1 corner sps; 127 sc between ch-1 sps)*

Rnds 44 & 45: Rep rnds 9 and 10. *(532 sts, 4 ch-1 corner sps; 133 sc between ch-1 sps)*

Rnd 46: With woodbine, rep rnd 11. *(532 sts, 4 5-tr corners; 133 sts between corners)*

Rnds 47 & 48: With greenhouse, rep rnds 12 and 13. *(556 sts, 4 3-sc corners; 139 sts between corners)*

Rnd 49: With woodbine, rep rnd 14. *(564 sts, 4 5-tr corners; 141 sts between corners)*

Rnd 50: Rep rnd 15. *(588 sts, 4 ch-1 corner sps; 147 sts between ch-1 sps)*

Rnds 51–59: Rep rnds 37–45. *(692 sts, 4 ch-1 corner sps; 173 sc between ch-1 sps)*

Rnd 60: With fawn mix, rep rnd 32. *(692 sts, 4 3-sc corners; 173 sts between corners)*

Rnd 61: Ch 3, *(2 dc, ch 1, 2 dc) in next ch-1 corner sp, dc in each of next 2 sc, [LC cable in next 3 sts] across to last 2 sts before next corner ch-1 sp**, dc in each of next 2 sts, rep from * around, ending last rep at **, dc in last st, join in top of beg ch-3. *(228 LC cables, 32 dc, 4 ch-1 corner sps; 57 LC cables, 8 dc between ch-1 sps)*

Rnd 62: Ch 3, dc in each of next 2 dc, *(2 dc, ch 1, 2 dc) in corner ch-1 sp, dc in each of next 4 dc, (RC cable in next 3 sts) to last 4 sts before corner**, dc in each of next 4 sts, rep from * around, ending last rep at **, dc in last dc, join in top of beg ch-3. *(228 RC cables, 48 dc, 4 ch-1 corner sps; 57 RC cables, 12 dc between ch-1 sps)*

Rnd 63: Rep rnd 35. *(4 3-sc corners; 183 sc between corners; 744 sc total)*

Rnd 64: With RS facing, sc join burnished heather in 2nd sp of any 3-sc corner, (ch 1, sc) in same st, *sc in each st to next corner**, (sc, ch 1, sc) in corner sp, rep from * around, ending last rep at **, join in beg sc, fasten off. *(748 sts, 4 3-sc corners; 187 sc between corners)*

Rnd 65: With RS facing, sc join cinnabar in any ch-1 corner sp, 2 sc in same sp, sc in each st to next corner, 3 sc in corner ch-1 sp, rep from * around, ending last rep at **, join in beg sc, fasten off. *(760 sts, 4 3-sc corners; 187 sc between corners)*

Rnd 66: With RS facing, sc join harvest in 2nd sc of any 3-sc corner, 2 sc in same st, *sc in **back lp** *(see Stitch Guide)* of next st, [sc in both lps of next st, sc in back lp of next st] around to center st of next corner**, 3 sc in center st, rep from * around, ending last rep at **, join in beg sc, fasten off. *(756 sts, 4 3-sc corners; 189 sc between corners)*

Rnd 67: With RS facing, sc join cinnabar in 2nd sc of any 3-sc corner, 2 sc in same st, *sk next st, [(sc, ch 1, sc) in next st, sk next st *(Photo 22)*] around to center st of next corner, 3 sc in center st, rep from * around, ending last rep at **, join in beg sc, fasten off. *(768 sts, 4 3-sc corners; 190 sc between corners)*

Photo 22

SERENITY MANDALA THROW

Rich textures combine with a soothing neutral palette to create a throw that's cozy and calming. Post stitch rounds form raised ridges that create dimensional contrast with the openwork rounds.

①②③④⑤⑥ **INTERMEDIATE**

FINISHED MEASUREMENT

52 inches in diameter

MATERIALS

- Red Heart Hygge bulky (chunky) weight acrylic/nylon yarn (5 oz/132yds/141g per skein):
    3 skeins each #8334 almond, #8406 pearl and #8339 cloud
    2 skeins #8369 latte
- Size K/10½/6.5mm or size needed to obtain gauge
- Tapestry needle

GAUGE

10 tr = 4 inches; rnds 1–6 = 5 inches

Gauge is not essential to this project.

PATTERN NOTES

Throw is worked in rounds.

Color changes are made by fastening off first color and joining new color as indicated. Weave in loose ends as work progresses.

Join with slip stitch unless otherwise stated.

Chain-4 at beginning of round counts as first double crochet and chain-1 space unless otherwise stated.

Chain-4 at beginning of round counts as first back post double crochet and chain-1 space unless otherwise stated.

Chain-4 at beginning of round counts as first treble crochet unless otherwise stated.

Chain-2 at beginning of round counts as first half double crochet unless otherwise stated.

Chain-3 at beginning of round counts as first double crochet unless otherwise stated.

Chain-1 at beginning of round counts as first single crochet unless otherwise stated.

Chain-8 at beginning of round counts as first single crochet and chain-7 space unless otherwise stated.

Chain-3 at beginning of round counts as first back post double crochet unless otherwise stated.

Chain-5 at beginning of round counts as first double crochet and chain-2 space unless otherwise stated.

Chain-6 at beginning of round counts as first single crochet and chain-5 space unless otherwise stated.

At end of rounds 7 and 22, a treble crochet stitch is used as a bridge stitch to complete the round and bring the hook to the desired position.

SPECIAL STITCHES

Beginning treble crochet decrease (beg tr dec): Ch 3, tr in indicated st.

Treble crochet decrease (tr dec): Yo twice, insert hook in indicated st, yo, pull through st, [yo, pull through 2 lps on hook] twice, yo twice, insert hook in indicated st, yo, pull through st, [yo, pull through 2 lps on hook] twice, yo and pull through all 3 lps on hook.

Single crochet join (sc join): Place slip knot on hook, insert hook in indicated st, yo and draw up lp, yo and pull through both lps on hook.

THROW

Rnd 1 (RS): With almond, ch 5, **join** *(see Pattern Notes)* in first ch to form ring, **ch 4** *(see Pattern Notes)*, [dc in ring, ch 1] 7 times, join in 3rd ch of beg ch-4. Fasten off. *(8 dc, 8 ch-1 sps)*

Rnd 2: Join pearl in any st, **ch 2** *(see Pattern Notes)*, 2 hdc in next sp, [hdc in next st, 2 hdc in next sp] around, join in top of beg ch-2. Fasten off. *(24 hdc)*

Rnd 3: Join latte in **back bar** *(see illustration)* of any hdc, **ch 3** *(see Pattern Notes)*, 2 dc in back bar of next st, [dc in back bar of next st, 2 dc in back bar of next st] around, join in top of beg ch-3. Fasten off. *(36 dc)*

Half Double Crochet Back Bar
(illustration shows side facing away from stitcher)

Rnd 4: Working from back, join cloud around post of any st, ch 4 *(counts as bptr, ch 1)*, [**bptr** *(see Stitch Guide)* around next st, ch 1] around, join in 3rd ch of beg ch-4. Fasten off. *(36 bptr, 36 ch-1 sps)*

Rnd 5: Join almond in any sp, **ch 4** *(see Pattern Notes)*, tr in same sp, 2 tr in each rem sp around, join in top of beg ch-4. *(72 tr)*

Rnd 6: Ch 1 *(see Pattern Notes)*, sc in each st around, join in beg ch-1. Fasten off. *(72 sc)*

Rnd 7: Join pearl in any st, [ch 4, sk next st, tr in next st, ch 4, sk next st, sl st in next st] 17 times, ch 4, sk next st, tr in next st, sk next st, **tr in same st as beg ch-4** *(see Pattern Notes)*. *(19 tr, 36 sps, 18 sl sts)*

Rnd 8: Ch 8 *(see Pattern Notes)*, [sc in next tr, ch 7] around, join in first ch of beg ch-8. *(18 sc, 18 ch-7 sps)*

Rnd 9: Sl st in first ch-7 sp, ch 3, 6 dc in same sp, 7 dc in each rem ch-7 sp around, join in top of beg ch-3. Fasten off. *(126 dc)*

Rnd 10: Working from back, join latte around post of any st from behind, **ch 3** *(see Pattern Notes)*, bptr around each st around, join in top of beg ch-3. *(126 bptr)*

Rnd 11: Beg tr dec *(see Special Stitches)* in same ch as join, ch 2, sk next st, [**tr dec** *(see Special Stitches)* in next st, ch 2, sk next st] around, join in top of beg ch-3. Fasten off. *(63 tr dec, 63 ch-2 sps)*

Rnd 12: Join cloud in any sp, ch 3, dc in same sp, 2 dc in each rem sp around, join in top of beg ch-3. *(126 dc)*

Rnd 13: Ch 5 *(see Pattern Notes)*, sk next st, [dc in next st, ch 2, sk next st] around, join in 3rd ch of beg ch-5. Fasten off. *(63 dc, 63 ch-2 sps)*

Rnd 14: Sc join *(see Special Stitches)* almond in any sp, 2 sc in same sp, 3 sc in each sp around, join in beg sc. *(189 sc)*

Rnd 15: Ch 4, tr in each st around, join in top of beg ch-4. Fasten off.

Rnd 16: Working from back, join pearl around post of any st from behind, ch 3, bptr around each st around, join in top of beg ch-3.

Rnd 17: Ch 1, sc in each st around, join in beg ch. Fasten off.

Rnd 18: Join latte in any st, ch 4, tr in next st, ch 2, sk next st, [tr in each of next 2 sts, ch 2, sk next st] around, join in top of beg ch-4. *(126 tr, 63 ch-2 sps)*

Rnd 19: Ch 3, dc in each st and 2 dc in each ch-2 sp around, join in top of beg ch-3. Fasten off. *(252 dc)*

Rnd 20: Join cloud in any st, ch 3, dc in each st around, join in top of beg ch-3.

Rnd 21: Ch 1, sc in each st around, join in beg ch. Fasten off.

Rnd 22: Join almond in any st, [ch 4, sk next st, tr in next st, ch 4, sk next st, sl st in next st] 62 times, ch 4, sk next st, tr in next st, sk next st, tr in same st as beg ch-4. *(64 tr, 126 sps, 63 sl sts)*

Rnd 23: Ch 6 *(see Pattern Notes)*, [sc in next tr, ch 5] around, join in first ch of beg ch-6. *(63 sc, 63 ch-5 sps)*

Rnd 24: Sl st in first ch-5 sp, ch 3, 4 dc in same sp, 5 dc in each rem ch-5 sp around, join in top of beg ch-3. Fasten off. *(315 dc)*

Rnd 25: Working from back, join pearl around post of any st from behind, ch 3, bptr around each st around, join in top of beg ch-3.

Rnd 26: Beg tr dec in same ch as joining, ch 2, sk next st, [tr dec in next 2 sts, ch 2, sk next st] around, join in top of beg ch-3. Fasten off. *(105 tr dec, 105 ch-2 sps)*

Rnd 27: Join latte in any sp, ch 3, 2 dc in same sp, 3 dc in each rem sp around, join in top of beg ch-3. *(315 dc)*

Rnd 28: Ch 4, sk next dc, [dc in each of next 2 dc, ch 1, sk next dc] around, dc in last dc, join in 3rd ch of beg ch-4. Fasten off. *(210 dc, 105 ch sps)*

Rnd 29: Sc join cloud in any sp, sc in each st and sp around, join in beg sc. *(315 sc)*

Rnd 30: Ch 4, tr in each st around, join in top of beg ch-4. Fasten off.

Rnd 31: Working from back, join almond around post of any st, ch 3, bptr around each st around, join in top of beg ch-3.

Rnd 32: Ch 4, tr in next st, ch 1, sk next st, [tr in each of next 2 sts, ch 1, sk next st] around, join in top of beg ch-4. Fasten off. *(210 tr, 105 sps)*

Rnd 33: Join pearl in any sp, ch 4, dc in same sp, dc in each of next 2 dc, [(dc, ch 1, dc) in next sp, dc in each of next 2 dc] around, join in 3rd ch of beg ch-4. Fasten off. *(420 dc, 105 ch-1 sps)*

Rnd 34: Join cloud in any sp, ch 3, dc in same sp, [bpdc around each of next 4 dc, 2 dc in next ch-1 sp] around, bpdc around each of last 4 dc, join in top of beg ch-3. Fasten off. *(420 bpdc, 210 dc)*

SQUARED-UP MANDALA

New to mandala-style throws? Start with this simple-to-stitch throw. Worked in self-striping worsted-weight yarn using easy stitches, you'll not only enjoy making this afghan, but you will be ready to take on your next project too!

EASY

FINISHED MEASUREMENT
45½ inches square

MATERIALS

4 MEDIUM

- Caron Big Cakes medium (worsted) weight acrylic yarn (10½ oz/603 yds/300g per cake):
    3 cakes #10527482 toffee brickle
- Size J/10/6mm crochet hook or size needed to obtain gauge
- Tapestry needle

GAUGE
In pattern: 4 rnds = 4 inches in diameter

PATTERN NOTES
Blanket is worked from the center out in rounds.

Slip stitch into the first chain-2 space at the beginning of each round.

Chain-4 at beginning of round counts as first double crochet and chain-2 unless otherwise stated.

Chain-2 at beginning of round counts as first double crochet.

Chain-3 at beginning of round counts as first double crochet and chain-1 space. This double crochet and chain-1 space plus the next double crochet creates the starting V-stitch of the next round.

Join with a slip stitch unless otherwise stated.

SPECIAL STITCHES
Fan: 7 dc in indicated sp.

V-stitch (V-st): (Dc, ch 1, dc) in indicated st.

Popcorn (pc): Work 4 hdc in indicated st, remove hook, insert hook in first hdc, pull lp through, ch 1.

Mini berry stitch (mini berry st): Insert hook into indicated st, yo, pull lp through, [yo, pull through first lp on hook] 3 times, yo, pull through rem 2 lps.

Cluster (cl): [Yo, insert hook into indicated sp, yo, pull lp through, yo, pull through 2 lps on hook] 3 times, yo, pull through rem 4 lps.

THROW

SECTION 1

Rnd 1: Ch 4, **join** *(see Pattern Notes)* in first ch to form a ring.

Rnd 2: Ch 4 *(see Pattern Notes)*, [**V-st** *(see Special Stitches)* in ring, ch 2] 3 times, dc in ring, ch 1, join in 2nd ch of beg ch-4. *(4 V-sts)*

Rnd 3: Sl st into ch-2 sp *(see Pattern Notes)*, ch 1, sc in same ch-2 sp, * **fan** *(see Special Stitches)* in next ch-1 sp of V-st**, sc in next ch-2 sp; rep from * around, ending last rep at **, join in beg sc. *(4 fans)*

Rnd 4: Ch 4, V-st in first sc, *ch 5**, (V-st, ch 2, V-st) in next sc; rep from * around, ending last rep at **, dc in first sc, ch 1, join in 2nd ch of beg ch-4. *(8 V-sts, 4 ch-5 sps, 4 ch-2 sps)*

Rnd 5: Ch 2, 2 dc in same ch-2 sp, ch 1, 3 dc in same ch-2 sp, *ch 1, working over ch-5 sp, 3 dc in 4th dc of fan, ch 1**, (3 dc, ch 2, 3 dc) in ch-2 sp; rep from * around, ending last rep at **, join in top of beg ch-2. *(12 3-dc groups, 8 ch-1 sps, 4 ch-2 sps)*

Rnds 6–11: Ch 2, 2 dc in same ch-2 sp, ch 1, 3 dc in same ch-2 sp, *ch 1, [3 dc in next ch-1 sp, ch 1**] across to ch-2 sp, (3 dc, ch 2, 3 dc) in ch-2 sp; rep from * around, ending last rep at **, join in top of beg ch-2. *(36 3-dc groups, 32 ch-1 sps, 4 ch-2 sps)*

Rnd 12: Ch 4, dc in same ch-2 sp, *ch 1, [dc in 2nd dc of 3-dc group, ch 1**, dc in next ch-1 sp, ch 1] across to ch-2 sp, ending last rep at **, (dc, ch 2, dc) in ch-2 sp; rep from * around, ending last rep at **, join in 2nd ch of beg ch-4. *(76 dc, 72 ch-1 sps, 4 ch-2 sps)*

SECTION 2

Rnd 13: Ch 1, (sc, ch 2, sc) in same ch-2 sp, *ch 1, [sc in next ch-1 sp, ch 1**] across to ch-2 sp, (sc, ch 2, sc) in ch-2 sp; rep from * around, ending last rep at **, join in beg sc. *(80 sc, 76 ch-1 sps, 4 ch-2 sps)*

Rnd 14: Ch 4, dc in same ch-2 sp, *ch 1, [**dc dec** *(see Stitch Guide)* in same ch sp as previous st and in next ch sp, ch 1] across to next ch-2 sp, dc dec in same ch sp as previous st and in next ch-2 sp, ch 1**, (dc, ch 2, dc) in ch-2 sp; rep from * around, ending last rep at **, join in 2nd ch of beg ch-4. *(80 dc dec, 84 ch-1 sps, 8 dc, 4 ch-2 sps)*

Rnd 15: Ch 1, (sc, ch 2, sc) in same ch-2 sp, *ch 1, [sc in next ch-1 sp, ch 1**] across to ch-2 sp, (sc, ch 2, sc) in ch-2 sp; rep from * around, ending last rep at **, join in beg sc. *(92 sc, 88 ch-1 sps, 4 ch-2 sps)*

Rnds 16–23: [Rep rnds 14 and 15] 4 times. *(140 sc, 136 ch-1 sps, 4 ch-2 sps)*

SECTION 3

Rnd 24: Ch 2 *(doesn't count as a st)*, (hdc, ch 2, hdc) in same ch-2 sp, *[**pc** *(see Special Stitches)* in next sc, hdc in next ch-1 sp, in next sc and in next ch-1 sp] across to last sc before ch-2 sp, pc in last sc**, (hdc, ch 1, hdc) in ch-2 sp; rep from * around, ending last rep at **, join in top of beg hdc. *(72 pc, 212 hdc, 4 ch-2 sps)*

Rnd 25: Ch 4, dc in same ch-2 sp, *ch 1, sk first st, [dc in next st, ch 1, sk next st**] across to ch-2 sp, (dc, ch 2, dc) in ch-2 sp; rep from * around, ending last rep at **, join in 2nd ch of beg ch-4. *(148 dc, 144 ch-1 sps, 4 ch-2 sps)*

Rnd 26: Ch 1, (sc, ch 2, sc) in same ch-2 sp, * **mini berry st** *(see Special Stitches)* in first dc, [sc in next ch-1 sp, mini berry st in next dc**] across to ch-2 sp, (sc, ch 2, sc) in ch-2 sp; rep from * around, ending last rep at **, join in beg sc. *(148 mini berry sts, 152 sc, 4 ch-2 sps)*

Rnd 27: Ch 4, dc in same ch-2 sp, *ch 1, dc in first mini berry st, ch 1, [dc in next mini berry st, ch 1**] across to ch-2 sp, (dc, ch 2, dc) in ch-2 sp; rep from * around, ending last rep at **, join in 2nd ch of beg ch-4. *(156 dc, 152 ch-1 sps, 4 ch-2 sps)*

Rnds 28–31: [Rep rnds 26 and 27] twice. *(172 dc, 168 ch-1 sps, 4 ch-2 sps)*

Rnd 32: Ch 2 *(doesn't count as a st)*, (hdc, ch 2, hdc) in same ch-2 sp, *pc in first st, [hdc in next 3 sts, pc in next st**] across to ch-2 sp, (hdc, ch 2, hdc) in ch-2 sp; rep from * around, ending last rep at **, join in top of beg hdc. *(88 pc, 260 hdc, 4 ch-2 sps)*

SECTION 4

Rnd 33: Ch 1, (sc, ch 2, sc) in same ch-2 sp, *ch 1, sk next st, [sc in next st, ch 1, sk next st**] across to ch-2 sp, (sc, ch 2, sc) in ch-2 sp; rep from * around, ending last rep at **, join in beg sc. *(180 sc, 176 ch-1 sps, 4 ch-2 sps)*

Rnd 34: Rep rnd 15. *(184 sc, 180 ch-1 sps, 4 ch-2 sps)*

Rnd 35: Ch 4, dc in same ch-2 sp, *ch 1, **cl** *(see Special Stitches)* in next ch sp, [ch 1, dc in next ch sp, ch 1, cl in next ch sp, ch 1**] across to ch-2 sp, (dc, ch 2, dc) in ch-2 sp; rep from * around, ending last rep at **, join in 2nd ch of beg ch-4. *(92 cls, 96 dc, 184 ch-1 sps, 4 ch-2 sps)*

Rnds 36–46: [Rep rnds 34 and 35] 5 times and rnd 34 once. *(232 sc, 228 ch-1 sps, 4 ch-2 sps)*

SECTION 5

Rnd 47: Ch 4, dc in same ch-2 sp, *V-st in first ch-1 sp, [dc in next ch-1 sp, V-st in next ch-1 sp] across to ch-2 sp, (dc, ch 2, dc) in ch-2 sp; rep from * around, ending last rep at **, join in 2nd ch of beg ch-4. *(116 V-sts, 120 dc, 4 ch-2 sps)*

Rnd 48: Ch 4, dc in same ch-2 sp, *dc in first dc, [V-st in ch-1 sp of next V-st, dc in next dc**] across to ch-2 sp, (dc, ch 2, dc) in ch-2 sp; rep from * around, ending last rep at **, join in 2nd ch of beg ch-4. *(116 V-sts, 128 dc, 4 ch-2 sps)*

Rnd 49: Ch 3 *(see Pattern Notes)*, (dc, ch 2, dc, ch 1, dc) in same ch-2 sp, *sk first dc, dc in next dc, V-st in ch-1 sp of next V-st, dc in next dc**] across to 1 st before ch-2 sp, sk next dc, (dc, ch 1, dc, ch 2, dc, ch 1, dc) in ch-2 sp; rep from * around, ending last rep at **, join in 2nd ch of beg ch-4. *(116 V-sts, 136 dc, 8 ch-1 sps, 4 ch-2 sps)*

Rnd 50: Ch 4, dc in same ch-2 sp, *V-st in ch-1 sp of first V-st, [dc in next dc, V-st in ch-1 sp of next V-st**] across to ch-2 sp, (dc, ch 2, dc) in ch-2 sp; rep from * around, ending last rep at **, join in 2nd ch of beg ch-4. *(124 V-sts, 120 dc, 4 ch-2 sps)*

Rnds 51–53: [Rep rnds 48–50] once. *(132 V-sts, 128 dc, 4 ch-2 sps)*

BORDER

Rnd 54: Ch 4, dc in same ch-2 sp, *ch 1, dc in ch-1 sp of first V-st, ch 1, [dc in next dc, ch 1, dc in ch-1 sp of next V-st, ch 1**] across to ch-2 sp, (dc, ch 2, dc) in ch-2 sp; rep from * around, ending last rep at **, join in 2nd ch of beg ch-4. *(268 dc, 264 ch-1 sps, 4 ch-2 sps)*

Rnd 55: Rep rnd 26. Fasten off. *(268 mini berry sts, 272 sc, 4 ch-2 sps)*

STARBURST MANDALA THROW

Highly textured relief stitches make this round mandala design pop! Deep teal sets off this design worked in worsted-weight yarn.

①②③④⑤⑥ **INTERMEDIAT**

FINISHED MEASUREMENT

48 inches in diameter

MATERIALS

[4 MEDIUM]

- Premier Yarns Basix medium (worsted) weight acrylic yarn (7 oz/359 yds/200g per skein):
    6 skeins #1115-45 teal
- Size H/8/5mm crochet hook or size needed to obtain gauge
- Sizes G/6/4mm and I/9/5.5mm crochet hooks
- Tapestry needle

GAUGE

Rnds 1–7 in pattern with H hook = 4¼ inches in diameter

PATTERN NOTES

Weave in ends as work progresses.

At the end of a round, join with slip stitch in first stitch unless otherwise stated.

Chain-3 at beginning of round counts as first double crochet unless otherwise stated.

In stitch counts, post stitches and decrease stitches are listed as a regular stitch. A front post double crochet is included in the double crochet stitch count and so on.

This pattern features a stitch called the "knuckle stitch." The first round of the stitch is worked on the back side of the piece and is comprised of (single crochet, treble crochet in the back loop only). Because of the difference in stitch height, the treble crochet bends backwards, something like a knuckle. The 2nd round of the stitch is worked from the right side. The hook is inserted into the top of the treble crochet and then into the unworked loop at the base of the treble crochet to lock the stitch into place.

SPECIAL STITCH

Knuckle Stitch (KS): Insert hook into indicated tr and into unworked lp of st at its base, yo, pull up a lp, yo, pull through 2 lps *(sc made)*.

THROW

With H hook, ch 5; join with a sl st in the first ch to form a ring.

Rnd 1: Ch 3 *(see Pattern Notes)*, 11 dc in the ring, **join** *(see Pattern Notes)*, ch 1; turn. *(12 dc)*

Rnd 2 (WS): Working in **back lps** only *(see Stitch Guide)*, (sc, tr) in each dc around, join, ch 1; turn. *(24 sts)*

Rnd 3 (RS): KS *(see Special Stitch)* in first tr, ch 1, sk next sc, [KS in next tr, ch 1, sk next sc] around, join. *(12 KS, 12 ch-1 sps)*

Rnd 4: Ch 1, sc in first st, ch 1, sc in the next ch-1 sp, ch 1, [sc in the next st, ch 1, sc in the next ch-1 sp, ch 1] 11 times, join. *(24 sc, 24 ch-1 sps)*

Rnd 5: Sl st into the first ch-1 sp, ch 1, sc in the same ch-1 sp, ch 1, sk next sc, [sc in the next ch-1 sp, ch 1, sk next sc] 23 times, join, ch 1; turn.

Rnd 6: Sc in the first ch-1 sp, tr in back lp only of next sc, [sc in the next ch-1 sp, tr in back lp only of next sc] 23 times, join, ch 1; turn. *(48 sts)*

Rnd 7: Rep rnd 3. *(24 KS, 24 ch-1 sps)*

Rnd 8: Ch 3, dc in the next ch-1 sp, [dc in the next sc, dc in the next ch-1 sp] around, join. *(48 dc)*

Rnd 9: Ch 1 loosely, **fpdc** *(see Stitch Guide)* around first dc, fpdc around each of the next 2 dc, ch 1, sc in next dc, ch 1, [fpdc around each of next 3 dc, ch 1, sc in the next dc, ch 1] around, join. *(36 dc, 12 sc, 24 ch-1 sps)*

Rnd 10: Ch 1 loosely, fpdc around each of first 3 fpdc, [ch 1, sc in the next ch-1 sp] 2 times, ch 1, *fpdc around each of the next 3 fpdc, [ch 1, sc in the next ch-1 sp] 2 times, ch 1, rep from * around, join. *(36 dc, 24 sc, 36 ch-1 sps)*

Rnd 11: Ch 1 loosely, fpdc around each of first 3 fpdc, [ch 1, sc in the next ch-1 sp] 3 times, ch 1, *fpdc around each of next 3 fpdc, [ch 1, sc in the next ch-1 sp] 3 times, ch 1, rep from * around, join. *(36 dc, 36 sc, 48 ch-1 sps)*

Rnd 12: Ch 1 loosely, fpdc around the first fpdc, (dc, fpdc, dc) in next fpdc, fpdc around the next fpdc, [sc in the next ch-1 sp, ch 1] 3 times, sc in the next ch-1 sp, *fpdc around the next fpdc, (dc, fpdc, dc) in the next fpdc, fpdc around next fpdc, [sc in the next ch-1 sp, ch 1] 3 times, sc in the next ch-1 sp, rep from * around, join. *(60 dc, 48 sc, 36 ch-1 sps)*

Rnd 13: Ch 1 loosely, fpdc around the first fpdc, fpdc around the next dc, 2 dc in the next fpdc, fpdc around each of the next 2 sts, sk next sc, [sc in the next ch-1 sp, ch 1] 2 times, sc in the next ch-1 sp, sk next sc, *fpdc around each of the next 2 sts, 2 dc around the next fpdc, fpdc around each of the next 2 sts, sk next sc, [sc in the next ch-1 sp, ch 1] 2 times, sc in the next ch-1 sp, sk next sc, rep from * around, join. *(72 dc, 36 sc, 24 ch-1 sps)*

Rnd 14: Ch 1 loosely, fpdc around each of the first 2 fpdc, fpdc around the next dc, ch 1, fpdc around the next dc, fpdc around each of the next 2 fpdc, sk next sc, sc in the next ch-1 sp, ch 1, sc in the next ch-1 sp, sk next sc, *fpdc around each of the next 2 fpdc, fpdc around the next dc, ch 1, fpdc around the next dc, fpdc around each of the next 2 fpdc, sk next sc, sc in the next ch-1 sp, ch 1, sc in the next ch-1 sp, sk next sc, rep from * around, join. *(72 fpdc, 24 sc, 24 ch-1 sps)*

Rnd 15: Ch 1 loosely, fpdc around each of first 3 fpdc, ch 1, sc in next ch-1 sp, ch 1, fpdc around each of the next 3 fpdc, sk next sc, sc in next ch-1 sp, sk the next sc, *fpdc around each of the next 3 fpdc, ch 1, sc in the next ch-1 sp, ch 1, fpdc around each of next 3 fpdc, sk next sc, sc in next ch-1 sp, sk next sc, rep from * around, join.

Rnd 16: Ch 1 loosely, fpdc around each of the first 3 fpdc, [ch 1, sc in next ch-1 sp] 2 times, ch 1, fpdc around each of next 3 fpdc, sk next sc, *fpdc around each of next 3 fpdc, [ch 1, sc in the next ch-1 sp] 2 times, ch 1, fpdc around each of next 3 fpdc, sk the next sc, rep from * around, join. Fasten off. *(72 dc, 24 sc, 36 ch-1 sps)*

Rnd 17: Sk first 3 fpdc, join yarn with a sl st in the top of next fpdc, ch 1 loosely, fpdc around same fpdc, fpdc around next fpdc, **fpdc dec** *(see Stitch Guide)* in next 2 fpdc, fpdc around each of next 2 fpdc, [ch 1, sc in the next ch-1 sp] 3 times, ch 1, *fpdc around each of next 2 fpdc, fpdc dec in next 2 fpdc, fpdc around each of next 2 fpdc, [ch 1, sc in the next ch-1 sp] 3 times, ch 1, rep from * around, join. *(60 dc, 36 sc, 48 ch-1 sps)*

Rnd 18: Ch 1 loosely, fpdc dec in first 2 fpdc, fpdc around next st, fpdc dec in next 2 fpdc, [ch 1, sc in the next ch-1 sp] 4 times, ch 1, *fpdc dec in next 2 fpdc, fpdc around next st, fpdc dec in next 2 fpdc, [ch 1, sc in the next ch-1 sp] 4 times, ch 1, rep from * around, join. *(36 dc, 48 sc, 60 ch-1 sps)*

Rnd 19: Ch 1 loosely, fpdc around first 3 sts, [ch 1, sc in next ch-1 sp] 5 times, ch 1, *fpdc around each of next 3 sts, [ch 1, sc in the next ch-1 sp] 5 times, ch 1, rep from * around, join. *(36 dc, 60 sc, 72 ch-1 sps)*

Rnd 20: Ch 1 loosely, fpdc around each of first 3 fpdc, [ch 1, sc in next ch-1 sp] 6 times, ch 1, *fpdc around each of next 3 fpdc, [ch 1, sc in the next ch-1 sp] 6 times, ch 1, rep from * around, join. *(36 dc, 72 sc, 84 ch-1 sps)*

Rnd 21: Ch 1 loosely, fpdc around each of first 3 fpdc, [ch 1, sc in next ch-1 sp] 7 times, ch 1, *fpdc around each of next 3 fpdc, [ch 1, sc in the next ch-1 sp] 7 times, ch 1, rep from * around, join. *(36 dc, 84 sc, 96 ch-1 sps)*

Rnd 22: Ch 1 loosely, fpdc around first fpdc, ch 1, fptr around next fpdc, ch 1, fpdc around next fpdc, [ch 1, sc in the next ch-1 sp] 3 times, ch 1, sc dec in next

2 ch-1 sps, [ch 1, sc in the next ch-1 sp] 3 times, ch 1, *fpdc around next fpdc, ch 1, fptr around next fpdc, ch 1, fpdc around next fpdc, [ch 1, sc in the next ch-1 sp] 3 times, ch 1, sc dec in next 2 ch-1 sps, [ch 1, sc in the next ch-1 sp] 3 times, ch 1, rep from * around, join, ch 1, turn. *(24 dc, 12 tr, 84 sc, 120 ch-1 sps)*

Rnd 23 (WS): Sc in the first ch-1 sp, tr in back lps only of next st, [sc in next ch-1 sp, tr in back lps only of next st] around; join, ch 1; turn. *(120 tr, 120 sc)*

Rnd 24 (RS): KS in first tr, ch 1, sk next sc, [KS in next tr, ch 1, sk next sc] around; join. *(120 KS, 120 ch-1 sps)*

Rnd 25: Sl st into the first ch-1 sp, ch 1, sc in same ch-1 sp, *ch 1, sc in the next sc, [ch 1, sc in the next ch-1 sp] 4 times, ch 1, sc dec in next 2 ch-1 sps**, [ch 1, sc in the next ch-1 sp] 4 times, rep from * around, ending last rep at **, [ch 1, sc in the next ch-1 sp] 3 times, ch 1, join. *(120 sc, 120 ch-1 sps)*

Rnd 26: Sl st into the first ch-1 sp, ch 1, sc in the same ch-1 sp, *ch 1, sc in the next sc, [ch 1, sc in the next ch-1 sp] 10 times; rep from * 10 times, ch 1, sc in the next sc, [ch 1, sc in the next ch-1 sp] 9 times, ch 1, join. *(132 sc, 132 ch-1 sps)*

Rnd 27: Sl st into the first ch-1 sp, ch 1, sc in the same ch-1 sp, *ch 1, sc in the next sc, [ch 1, sc in the next ch-1 sp] 11 times; rep from * 10 times, ch 1, sc in the next sc, [ch 1, sc in the next ch-1 sp] 10 times, ch 1, join. *(144 sc, 144 ch-1 sps)*

Rnd 28: Sl st into the first ch-1 sp, ch 1, sc in the same ch-1 sp, *ch 1, sc in the next sc, [ch 1, sc in the next ch-1 sp] 5 times, ch 1, sc dec in next 2 ch-1 sps**, [ch 1, sc in next ch-1 sp] 5 times, rep from * around, ending last rep at **, [ch 1, sc in next ch-1 sp] 4 times, ch 1, join, ch 1; turn.

Rnds 29 & 30: Rep rnds 23 and 24. *(144 KS, 144 ch-1 sps)*

Rnd 31: Sl st into the first ch-1 sp, ch 1, sc in the same ch-1 sp, *ch 1, sc in the next sc, [ch 1, sc in the next ch-1 sp] 5 times, ch 1, sc dec in next 2 ch-1 sps**, [ch 1, sc in next ch-1 sp] 5 times, rep from * around, ending last rep at **, [ch 1, sc in next ch-1 sp] 4 times, ch 1, join. *(144 sc, 144 ch-1 sps)*

Rnd 32: Sl st into the first ch-1 sp, ch 1, sc in the same ch-1 sp, *ch 1, sc in next sc, [ch 1, sc in next ch-1 sp] 12 times; rep from * 10 times, ch 1, sc in next sc, [ch 1, sc in next ch-1 sp] 11 times, ch 1, join. *(156 sc, 156 ch-1 sps)*

Rnd 33: Sl st into the first ch-1 sp, ch 1, sc in same ch-1 sp, *ch 1, sc in next sc, [ch 1, sc in the next ch-1 sp] 13 times; rep from * 10 times, ch 1, sc in next sc, [ch 1, sc in next ch-1 sp] 12 times, ch 1, join. *(168 sc, 168 ch-1 sps)*

Rnd 34: Sl st into the first ch-1 sp, ch 1, sc in the same ch-1 sp, *ch 1, sc in the next sc, [ch 1, sc in the next ch-1 sp] 6 times, ch 1, sc dec in next 2 ch-1 sps**, [ch 1, sc in next ch-1 sp] 6 times, rep from * around, ending last rep at **, [ch 1, sc in next ch-1 sp] 5 times, ch 1, join, turn.

Rnds 35 & 36: Rep rnds 23 and 24. *(168 KS, 168 ch-1 sps)*

Rnd 37: Rep rnd 34, but do not turn at end of rnd.

Rnd 38: Sl st into the first ch-1 sp, ch 1, sc in same ch-1 sp, *ch 1, sc in next sc, [ch 1, sc in the next ch-1 sp] 14 times; rep from * 10 times, ch 1, sc in next sc, [ch 1, sc in next ch-1 sp] 13 times, ch 1, join. *(180 sc, 180 ch-1 sps)*

Rnd 39: Sl st into the first ch-1 sp, ch 1, sc in same ch-1 sp, *ch 1, sc in next sc, [ch 1, sc in the next ch-1 sp] 15 times; rep from * 10 times, ch 1, sc in next sc, [ch 1, sc in next ch-1 sp] 14 times, ch 1, join. *(192 sc, 192 ch-1 sps)*

Rnd 40: Sl st into the first ch-1 sp, ch 1, sc in the same ch-1 sp, *ch 1, sc in the next sc, [ch 1, sc in the next ch-1 sp] 7 times, ch 1, sc dec in next 2 ch-1 sps**, [ch 1, sc in next ch-1 sp] 7 times, rep from * around, ending last rep at **, [ch 1, sc in next ch-1 sp] 6 times, ch 1, join, ch 1; turn.

Rnds 41 & 42: Rep rnds 23 and 24. *(192 KS, 192 ch-1 sps)*

Rnd 43: Rep rnd 40, but do not turn at end of rnd.

Rnd 44: Sl st into the first ch-1 sp, ch 1, sc in same ch-1 sp, *ch 1, sc in next sc, [ch 1, sc in the next ch-1 sp] 16 times; rep from * 10 times, ch 1, sc in next sc, [ch 1, sc in next ch-1 sp] 15 times, ch 1, join. *(204 sc, 204 ch-1 sps)*

Rnd 45: Sl st into the first ch-1 sp, ch 1, sc in same ch-1 sp, *ch 1, sc in next sc, [ch 1, sc in the next ch-1 sp] 17 times; rep from * 10 times, ch 1, sc in next sc, [ch 1, sc in next ch-1 sp] 16 times, ch 1, join. *(216 sc, 216 ch-1 sps)*

Rnd 46: Sl st into the first ch-1 sp, ch 1, sc in the same ch-1 sp, *ch 1, sc in the next sc, [ch 1, sc in the next ch-1 sp] 8 times, ch 1, sc dec in next 2 ch-1 sps**, [ch 1, sc in next ch-1 sp] 8 times, rep from * around, ending last rep at **, [ch 1, sc in next ch-1 sp] 7 times, ch 1, join, ch 1; turn.

Rnds 47 & 48: Rep rnds 23 and 24. *(216 KS, 216 ch-1 sps)*

Rnd 49: Rep rnd 46, but do not turn at end of rnd.

Rnd 50: Sl st into the first ch-1 sp, ch 1, sc in same ch-1 sp, *ch 1, sc in next sc, [ch 1, sc in the next ch-1 sp] 18 times; rep from * 10 times, ch 1, sc in next sc, [ch 1, sc in next ch-1 sp] 17 times, ch 1, join. *(228 sc, 228 ch-1 sps)*

Rnd 51: Sl st into the first ch-1 sp, ch 1, sc in same ch-1 sp, *ch 1, sc in next sc, [ch 1, sc in the next ch-1 sp] 19 times; rep from * 10 times, ch 1, sc in next sc, [ch 1, sc in next ch-1 sp] 18 times, ch 1, join. *(240 sc, 240 ch-1 sps)*

Rnd 52: Sl st into the first ch-1 sp, ch 1, sc in the same ch-1 sp, *ch 1, sc in the next sc, [ch 1, sc in the next ch-1 sp] 9 times, ch 1, sc dec in next 2 ch-1 sps**, [ch 1, sc in next ch-1 sp] 9 times, rep from * around, ending last rep at **, [ch 1, sc in next ch-1 sp] 8 times, ch 1, join, ch 1; turn.

Rnds 53 & 54: Rep rnds 23 and 24. *(240 KS, 240 ch-1 sps)*

Rnd 55: Sl st into the first ch-1 sp, ch 3, dc in each of the next (KS, ch-1 sp), [ch 1, sc in the next ch-1 sp] 3 times, ch 1, *dc in each of the next (ch-1 sp, KS, ch-1 sp), [ch 1, sc in the next ch-1 sp] 3 times, ch 1, sk next KS, rep from * around, join. *(144 dc, 144 sc, 192 ch-1 sps)*

Rnd 56: Ch 1, *fpsc around each of next 3 dc, [sc in next ch-1 sp, ch 1] 3 times, sc in next ch-1 sp, fpdc around each of next 3 dc, [sc in next ch-1 sp, ch 1] 3 times, sc in next ch-1 sp, fptr around each of next 3 dc, [sc in next ch-1 sp, ch 1] 3 times, sc in next ch-1 sp, fpdc around each of next 3 dc, [sc in next ch-1 sp, ch 1] 3 times, sc in next ch-1 sp, rep from * around, join. *(36 sc, 72 dc, 36 tr, 192 sc, 144 ch-1 sps)*

Rnd 57: Ch 1 loosely, fpdc around each of the first 3 sts, [ch 1, sc in the next ch-1 sp] 3 times, ch 1, *fpdc around each of the next 3 sts, [ch 1, sc in the next ch-1 sp] 3 times, ch 1, rep from * around, join. *(144 dc, 144 sc, 192 ch-1 sps)*

Rnd 58: Ch 1 loosely, fpdc around each of the first 3 fpdc, [sc in the next ch-1 sp, ch 1] 3 times, sc in the next ch-1 sp, *fpdc around each of the next 3 fpdc, [sc in the next ch-1 sp, ch 1] 3 times, sc in the next ch-1 sp, rep from * around, join. *(144 dc, 192 sc, 144 ch-1 sps)*

Rnd 59: Rep rnd 57.

Rnd 60: Rep rnd 56.

Rnd 61: Rep rnd 57.

Rnds 62–65: [Rep rnds 58 and 59] 2 times. Change to I hook.

Rnds 66 & 67: Rep rnds 58 and 59.

Rnd 68: Rep rnd 58, ch 1; turn.

Rnd 69: Sc in the same fpdc as joining, *[tr in back lp only of next sc, sc in the next ch-1 sp] 3 times**, [tr in back lp only of next st, sc in the next st] 2 times, rep from * around, ending last rep at **, tr in back lp only of next st, sc in the next st, tr in back lp only of next st, join, ch 1; turn. *(240 tr, 240 sc)*

Rnd 70: Rep rnd 24. *(240 KS, 240 ch-1 sps)*

Rnds 71 & 72: Sl st into the first ch-1 sp, ch 1, sc in the same ch-1 sp, ch 1, sk next sc, [sc in the next ch-1 sp, ch 1, sk next sc] around; join, ch 1; turn.

Rnd 73: Rep rnd 23. *(240 tr, 240 sc)*

Rnd 74: Change to size G hook. KS in first tr, ch 3, sk next sc, [KS in next tr, ch 3, sk next sc] around, join. Fasten off. Weave in ends.

FINISHING

If necessary, steam to block.

CATHEDRAL ROSE WINDOW AFGHAN

Crocheted and assembled from the center out, this spectacular award-winning afghan is a true work of art. Take your time and enjoy making this beauty.

①②③④⑤⑥ **MODERATELY CHALLENGING**

FINISHED MEASUREMENT

Approximately 78 inches in diameter

MATERIALS

- Red Heart Super Saver medium (worsted) weight yarn (solids: 7 oz/364 yds/198g per skein; multis: 5 oz/236 yds/141g per skein):
    8 skeins #3955 wildflower
    7 skeins #312 black
    2 skeins #776 dark orchid
    1 skein #512 turquoise
- Size H/8/5mm crochet hook or size needed to obtain gauge
- Stitch markers
- Tapestry needle

GAUGE

Rnds 1 and 2 of Octagon = 2 inches;
4 dc = 1 inch; 2 dc rows = 1 inch
Rnds 1 and 2 of Pentagon = 2¼ inches

PATTERN NOTES

This afghan is created in sections. Always assemble pieces or join yarn with right side of work facing unless otherwise stated.

Chain-3 at beginning of double crochet row or round counts as first double crochet unless otherwise stated.

Join with slip stitch unless otherwise stated.

SPECIAL STITCHES

Increase (inc): 2 dc in next st.

Popcorn (pc): 3 dc in next st, drop lp from hook, insert hook in first dc of group, draw dropped lp through st, ch 1.

Double crochet decrease (dc dec): [Yo, insert hook in next st, pull up lp, yo, pull through 2 lps on hook] twice, yo, pull through 3 lps on hook.

AFGHAN

FIRST SECTION

Octagon

With wildflower, ch 4, **join** *(see Pattern Notes)* in first ch to form ring.

Rnd 1: Ch 3 *(see Pattern Notes)*, 11 dc in ring, join in top of ch-3. *(12 dc)*

Rnd 2: (Ch 3, dc) in first st, 2 dc in each st around, join in 3rd ch of beg ch-3. *(24 dc)*

Rnd 3: (Ch 4, dc) in first st *(beg ch-4 counts as first dc and ch-1 sp)*, dc in each of next 2 dc, *(dc, ch 1, dc) in next st, dc in each of next 2 sts, rep from * 6 times, join in 3rd ch of ch-4. *(32 dc, 8 ch-1 sps)*

Rnds 4 & 5: (Sl st, ch 4, dc) in first ch sp, *sk next st, dc in each st around to next ch-1 sp, (dc, ch 1, dc) in ch-1 sp, rep from * 6 times, sk next st, dc in each st around, join in 3rd ch of ch-4. Fasten off at end of rnd 5. *(40 dc, 48 dc)*

Rnd 6: Join black with sc in any ch-1 sp, sc in same ch sp, [sc in each of next 6 sts, 2 sc in next ch sp] 7 times, sc in each st around, join in first sc. Fasten off. *(64 sc)*

Pentagon

Make 8.

With dark orchid, ch 4, join in first ch to form ring.

Rnd 1: Ch 3, 11 dc in ring, join in top of ch-3. *(12 dc)*

Rnd 2: (Ch 3, 2 dc) in first st, 2 dc in each st around, join in 3rd ch of beg ch-3. *(25 dc)*

Rnd 3: Ch 3, (dc, ch 1, dc) in next st, *dc in each of next 4 sts, (dc, ch 1, dc) in next st, rep from * 3 times, dc in each of last 3 sts, join in 3rd ch of beg ch-3. Fasten off. *(30 sts)*

Rnd 4: Join black with sc in any ch-1 sp, sc in same ch sp (2 sc in same st form point), sc in each st around with 2 sc in each ch-1 sp, join in first sc. Fasten off. *(40 sc)*

Triangle

Make 8.

Row 1: With black, ch 19. Working in the top lp, sc in 2nd ch from hook, sc in each ch across, ch 1, sl st in end of ch-19, do not turn. *(18 sc)*

Row 2: Working on opposite side of foundation ch on row 1, sl st in each of first 3 chs, sc in each of next 2 chs, hdc in each of next 2 chs, dc in each of next 4 chs, hdc in each of next 2 chs, sc in each of next 2 chs, sl st in each of last 3 chs. Fasten off. *(18 sts)*

First Section Assembly

To assemble First Section, with black yarn, place pieces WS to WS and **whipstitch** *(see illustration)* through both layers, sew Pentagons around Octagon. Center each Triangle between 2 Pentagons with row 2 of Triangles facing Pentagons. Sew Triangles to Pentagons *(see First Section Assembly Diagram)*.

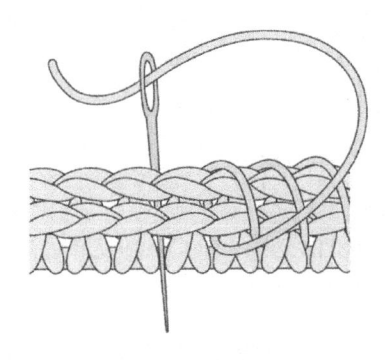

Whipstitch Edges

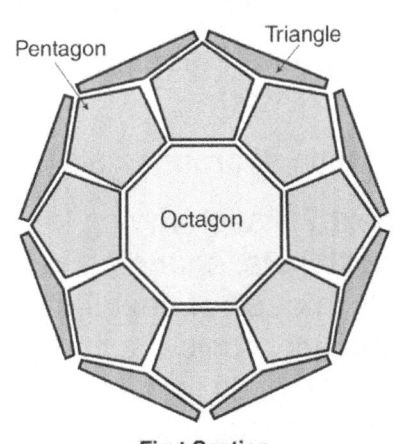

First Section Assembly Diagram

SECOND SECTION

Notes: For color changes in Second, Third and Fourth Sections, work over dropped yarn and, covering dropped yarn with sts, drop first color, with 2nd color, pull through last 2 lps of st. Always change to next color in last st made.

Rnd 1: Working around First Section, join black in one of the sc sts of any Pentagon point, (ch 3, dc) in same st as sl st, [sc in each of next 3 sts, hdc in each of next 3 sts, dc in each of next 6 sts, hdc in each of next 3 sts, sc in each of next 3 sts, 3 dc in sc of next Pentagon point] 7 times, sc in each of next 3 sts, dc in same st as ch-3, join in top of ch-3. *(168 sts)*

Rnd 2: Ch 3, dc in each of next 2 sts, **changing color to wildflower** *(see Second Section Notes) in last st*, dc in each of next 2 sts, **inc** *(see Special Stitches)*, dc in each of next 2 sts, changing to black, dc in each of next 5 sts, changing to wildflower, dc in each of next 6 sts, [changing to black, dc in each of next 5 sts, changing to wildflower, dc in each of next 2 sts, inc, dc in each of next 2 sts, changing to black, dc in each of next 5 sts, changing to wildflower, dc in each of next 6 sts] 7 times, changing to black at end of last rep, dc in each of last 2 sts, join in top of ch-3. *(176 sts)*

Rnd 3: Ch 3, dc in each of next 2 sts, changing to wildflower, dc in each of next 2 sts, inc, dc in each of next 3 sts, [changing to black, dc in each of next 5 sts, changing to wildflower, dc in each of next 2 sts, inc, dc in each of next 3 sts] 15 times, changing to black at end of last rep, dc in each of last 2 sts, join in 3rd ch of beg ch-3. *(192 sts)*

Rnd 4: Changing colors to match color sequence of last rnd, ch 3, dc in each st around with inc in second dc of each inc, join in top of ch-3. *(208 sts)*

Rnd 5: Changing colors to match color sequence of last rnd, ch 3, dc in each st around with inc in first dc of each inc, join in top of ch-3. *(224 sts)*

Rnds 6–8: Rep rnds 4 and 5 alternately, ending with rnd 4. At end of rnd 8, fasten off wildflower. *(240, 256, 272 sts)*

Rnd 9: With black, ch 3, dc in each st around, join in top of ch-3.

Rnd 10: Ch 3, dc in each of next 2 sts, changing to dark orchid, dc in each of next 2 sts, inc, dc in each of next 2 sts, changing to black, dc in each of next 2 sts, changing to dark orchid, dc in each of next 5 sts, [changing to black, dc in each of next 5 sts, changing to dark orchid, dc in each of next 2 sts, inc, dc in each of next 2 sts, changing to black, dc in each of next 2 sts, changing to dark orchid, dc in each of next 5 sts] 15 times, changing to black at end of last rep, dc in each of last 2 sts, join in top of ch-3. *(288 sts)*

Rnd 11: Ch 3, dc in each of next 2 sts, changing to dark orchid, dc in each of next 6 sts, changing to black, dc in each of next 2 sts, changing to dark orchid, dc in each of next 2 sts, inc, dc in each of next 2 sts, [changing to black, dc in each of next 5 sts, changing to dark orchid, dc in each of next 6 sts, changing to black, dc in each of next 2 sts, changing to dark orchid, dc in each of next 2 sts, inc, dc in each of next 2 sts] 15 times, changing to black at end of last rep, dc in each of last 2 sts, join in top of ch-3. Fasten off dark orchid. *(304 sts)*

Rnd 12: Ch 1, sc in each of first 3 sts, changing to turquoise, sc in next st, **pc** *(see Special Stitches)*, [sc in next st, pc] twice, changing to black at end of last rep, sc in each of next 2 sts, changing to turquoise, [sc in next st, pc] 3 times, changing to black at end of last rep, *sc in each of next 5 sts, changing to turquoise, [sc in next st, pc] 3 times, changing to black at end of last rep, sc in each of next 2 sts, changing to turquoise, [sc in next st, pc] 3 times, changing to black at end of last rep, rep from * 14 times, sc in each of last 2 sts, join in first sc. Fasten off turquoise.

Rnd 13: Sk ch-1 sp of each pc, ch 3, dc in each of next 2 sts, changing to wildflower, dc in each of next 6 sts, changing to black, dc in each of next 2 sts, changing to wildflower, dc in each of next 6 sts, [changing to black, dc in each of next 5 sts, changing to wildflower, dc in each of next 6 sts, changing to black, dc in each of next 2 sts, changing to wildflower, dc in each of next 6 sts] 15 times, changing to black at end of last rep, dc in each of last 2 sts, join in top of ch-3.

Rnd 14: Ch 3, dc in each of next 2 sts, changing to wildflower, dc in each of next 2 sts, inc, dc in each of next 3 sts, changing to black, dc in each of next 2 sts, changing to wildflower, dc in each of next 6 sts, [changing to black, dc in each of next 5 sts, changing to wildflower, dc in each of next 2 sts, inc, dc in each of next 3 sts, changing to black, dc in each of next 2 sts, changing to wildflower, dc in each of next 6 sts] 15 times, changing to black, dc in each of last 2 sts, join in top of ch-3. *(320 sts)*

Rnd 15: Ch 3, dc in each of next 2 sts, changing to wildflower, dc in each of next 7 sts, changing to black, dc in each of next 2 sts, changing to wildflower, dc in each of next 2 sts, inc, dc in each of next 3 sts, [changing to black, dc in each of next 5 sts, changing to wildflower, dc in each of next 7 sts, changing to black, dc in each of next 2 sts, changing to wildflower, dc in each of next 2 sts, inc, dc in each of next 3 sts] 15 times, changing to black at end of last rep, dc in each of last 2 sts, join in top of ch-3. *(336 sts)*

Rnd 16: Ch 3, dc in each of next 2 sts, changing to wildflower, dc in each of next 3 sts, inc, dc in each of next 3 sts, changing to black, dc in each of next 2 sts, changing to wildflower, dc in each of next 7 sts, [changing to black, dc in each of next 5 sts, changing to wildflower, dc in each of next 3 sts, inc, dc in each of next 3 sts, changing to black, dc in each of next 2 sts, changing to wildflower, dc in each of next 7 sts] 15 times, changing to black at end of last rep, dc in each of last 2 sts, join in top of ch-3. *(352 sts)*

Rnd 17: Ch 3, dc in each of next 2 sts, changing to wildflower, dc in each of next 8 sts, changing to black, dc in each of next 2 sts, changing to wildflower, dc in each of next 3 sts, inc, dc in each of next 3 sts, [changing to black, dc in each of next 5 sts, changing to wildflower, dc in each of next 8 sts, changing to black, dc in each of next 2 sts, changing to wildflower, dc in each of next 3 sts, inc, dc in each of next 3 sts] 15 times, changing to black at end of last rep, dc in each of last 2 sts, join in top of ch-3. Fasten off both colors. *(368 sts)*

Rnd 18: Sk first 3 black sts and next 8 wildflower sts before next black 2-dc group, [for Pyramid, sk next 2 black sts, join wildflower in first wildflower st past black 2-dc group, sc in next st, hdc in next st, dc in each of next 5 sts, changing to black, dc in each of next 5 sts, changing to wildflower, dc in each of next 5 sts, hdc in next st, sc in next st, sl st in last wildflower st of group, fasten off both colors] 16 times. *(16 Pyramids with 21 stsw each)*

Rnd 19: [Sk first 4 sts, join wildflower in next st, sc in next st, hdc in next st, dc in next st, changing to black, dc in each of next 5 sts, changing to wildflower, dc in next st, hdc in next st, sc in next st, sl st in next st, leaving last 4 sts unworked, fasten off both colors] in each Pyramid around. *(13 sts in each Pyramid)*

Rnd 20: For Columns *(make 1 in each Pyramid)*, work 9 rows as follows:

A: With WS of work facing, join black with sc in first black dc on Pyramid, sc in each of next 4 sts, leaving rem sts unworked, turn. *(5 sc)*

B: [Ch 1, sc in each st across, turn] 8 times for a total of 9 sc rows. At end of last row, fasten off. On last Column, do not fasten off.

Rnd 21: Ch 1, [sc in each of 5 sts across top of Column, ch 1, sc in end of each of next 9 rows, sc in each of next 18 unworked sts of rnds 17–19 to next Column, sc in end of next 9-row Column, ch 1] 16 times, join in first sc. Fasten off.

Large Heptagon

Make 16.

With wildflower, ch 4, join in first ch to form a ring.

Rnd 1: Ch 3, 13 dc in ring, join in top of ch-3. *(14 dc)*

Rnd 2: Ch 4 *(counts as first dc and ch-1 sp)*, dc in same st as beg ch-4, dc in next st, *(dc, ch 1, dc) in next st, dc in next st, rep from * 5 times, join in 3rd ch of ch-4. *(21 dc, 7 ch-1 sps)*

Rnds 3–5: (Sl st, ch 4, dc) in first ch sp, [dc in each st around to next ch-1 sp, (dc, ch 1, dc) in ch-1 sp] 6 times, dc in each st around, join in 3rd ch of ch-4. At end of rnd 5, fasten off. *(35 dc, 49 dc, 63 dc)*

Rnd 6: Join black with sc in any ch-1 sp, sc in each st and in each ch sp around, join in first sc. Fasten off. *(70 sc)*

Second Section Assembly

Matching corners, sew Large Heptagons to last rnd of Second Section between Columns *(see Assembly Diagram)*.

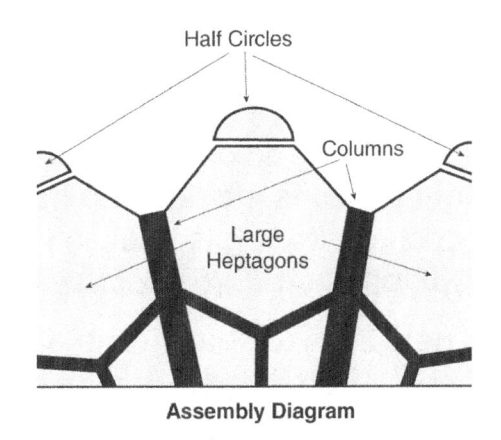

THIRD SECTION

Rnd 1: Working around entire afghan, spacing sts evenly, join black with sc in first st of any Column, sc in each of next 4 sts, 9 sc up side of next Large Heptagon, 2 sc in corner st, 9 sc across top of Large Heptagon, mark 4th st of last 9 sc made, 2 sc in next corner st, 9 sc down side of Large Heptagon, [sc in each of next 5 sts across top of Column, 9 sc up side of next Large Heptagon, 2 sc in corner st, 9 sc across top of Large Heptagon, mark 4th st of last 9 sc made, 2 sc in next corner st, 9 sc down side of Large Heptagon] 15 times, join in first sc. Fasten off. *(576 sc)*

Rnd 2: For Half Circle, work 3 rows as follows:

A: With dark orchid, join with sc in next marked st, sk next st, (3 dc, ch 1, 3 dc) in next st, sk next st, sc in each of next 3 sts, turn. *(10 sts, 1 ch sp)*

B: 3 dc in 2nd dc of next 3-dc group, ch 1, 3 dc in next ch sp, ch 1, 3 dc in 2nd dc of next 3-dc group, sk next st on rnd 1 of Third Section, sc in each of next 3 sts, turn. *(3 dc groups, 2 ch sps, 3 sc)*

C: 3 dc in 2nd dc of each 3-dc group and in each ch sp across, sk next st on rnd 1 of Third Section, sl st in next st. Fasten off. *(15 dc)*

D: [Rep steps A–C consecutively] 15 times for a total of 16 Half Circles.

Rnd 3: Working on rnd 1, join black in first st of any column, ch 3, *dc in each of next 3 sts, **dc dec** *(see Special Stitches)*, sc in each of next 9 sts including worked st, working across Half Circle in dc only, sk first sc, [sc in each of next 3 sts, 2 sc in next st] 3 times, sc in each of next 3 sts, working on rnd 1, sc in each of next 9 sts including worked st **, dc dec, rep from * 15 times, ending last rep at **, sk last st, join in top of beg ch-3. *(41 sts in each rep, 656 sts total)*

Rnd 4: Ch 3, [dc in each of next 3 sts, dc dec, hdc in each of next 12 sts, 2 hdc in next st, hdc in each of next 8 sts, 2 hdc in next st, hdc in each of next 12 sts, dc dec] 15 times, dc in each of next 3 sts, dc dec, hdc in each of next 12 sts, 2 hdc in next st, hdc in each of next 8 sts, 2 hdc in next st, hdc in each of next 12 sts, sk last st, join in top of ch-3.

Rnd 5: Ch 3, *dc in each of next 3 sts, dc dec, [dc in each of next 8 sts, 2 dc in next st] 3 times, dc in each of next 7 sts, dc dec, rep from * 14 times, dc in each of next 3 sts, dc dec, [dc in each of next 8 sts, 2 dc in next st] 3 times, dc in each of next 7 sts, sk next st, join in top of ch-3. *(672 sts)*

Rnd 6: Ch 3, *dc in each of next 3 sts, dc dec, [dc in each of next 11 sts, 2 dc in next st] twice, dc in each of next 11 sts, mark 9th st of last 11 dc made, dc dec, rep from * 14 times, dc in each of next 3 sts, dc dec, [dc in each of next 11 sts, 2 dc in next st] twice, dc in each of next 11 sts, mark 9th st of last 11 dc made, sk last st, join in top of ch-3. Fasten off.

Rnd 7: You now have a series of Points and Valleys. Fill in the Valleys as follows:

A: Join wildflower in marked st at bottom of next Valley *(sl sts do not count as sts)*, sc in next st, hdc in next st, changing to black, dc in each of next 5 sts, changing to wildflower, hdc in next st, sc in each of next 3 sts, sl st in next st, turn. *(11 sts)*

Note: *In steps B–H, work over sl sts into row below.*

B: Changing colors as established for remainder of rnd, sk sl st, sc in next st, hdc in next st, dc dec, dc in each of next 5 sts, dc dec, hdc in next st on rnd 6, sc in each of next 3 sts, sl st in next st, turn. *(13 sts)*

C: Sk sl st, sc in next st, hdc in next st, dc dec, dc in each of next 7 sts, dc dec, hdc in next st on rnd 6, sc in each of next 3 sts, sl st in next st, turn. *(15 sts)*

D: Sk sl st, sc in next st, hdc in next st, dc in next st, dc dec, dc in each of next 7 sts, dc dec, dc in next st, hdc in next st on rnd 6, sc in each of next 3 sts, sl st in next st, turn. *(17 sts)*

E: Sk sl st, sc in next st, hdc in next st, dc in each of next 2 sts, dc dec, dc in each of next 7 sts, dc dec, dc in each of next 2 sts, hdc in next st on rnd 6, sc in each of next 3 sts, sl st in next st, turn. *(19 sts)*

F: Sk sl st, sc in next st, hdc in next st, dc in each of next 3 sts, dc dec, dc in each of next 7 sts, dc dec, dc in each of next 3 sts, hdc in next st on rnd 6, sc in each of next 3 sts, sl st in next st, turn. *(21 sts)*

G: Sk sl st, sc in next st, hdc in next st, dc in each of next 4 sts, dc dec, dc in each of next 7 sts, dc dec, dc in each of next 4 sts, hdc in next st on rnd 6, sc in each of next 3 sts, sl st in next st. Fasten off. *(23 sts)*

H: [Rep steps A–G consecutively] 15 times to fill all 16 Valleys.

Rnd 8: Join black in first st of any black 5-dc group, ch 3, dc in each of next 4 sts, [changing to wildflower, dc in each of next 6 sts, inc, dc in each of next 3 sts, working across rnd 6, working over sl sts, dc in next st, changing to black, dc in each of next 5 sts, changing to wildflower, dc in each of next 2 sts, working across Valley fill-in, dc in next st, inc, dc in each of next 3 sts, inc, dc in each of next 2 sts *, changing to black, dc in each of next 5 sts] 16 times, ending last rep at *, changing to black, join in top of beg ch-3. *(34 sts in each rep—544 sts total)*

Rnd 9: Ch 3, dc in each of next 4, [changing to wildflower, dc in each of next 6 sts, inc, dc in each of next 5 sts, changing to black, dc in each of next 5 sts] 31 times, changing to wildflower, dc in each of next 6 sts, inc, dc in each of next 5 sts, changing to black, join in top of ch-3. *(576 sts)*

Rnd 10: Changing colors as established, ch 3, dc in each st around, join in top of ch-3.

Rnd 11: Ch 3, dc in each of next 4 sts, [changing to wildflower, dc in each of next 6 sts, inc, dc in each of next 6 sts, changing to black, dc in each of next 5 sts] 31 times, changing to wildflower, dc in each of next 6 sts, inc, dc in each of next 6 sts, changing to black, join in top of ch-3. Fasten off wildflower. *(608 sts)*

Rnd 12: With black, ch 3, dc in each st around, join in 3rd ch of beg ch-3.

Rnd 13: Ch 3, dc in each of next 4 sts, [changing to dark orchid, dc in each of next 6 sts, changing to black, dc in each of next 2 sts, changing to dark orchid, dc in each of next 6 sts, changing to black, dc in each of next 5 sts] 31 times, changing to dark orchid, dc in each of next 6 sts, changing to black, dc in each of next 2 sts, changing to dark orchid, dc in each of next 6 sts, changing to black, join in 3rd ch of beg ch-3.

Rnd 14: Ch 3, dc in each of next 4 sts, [changing to dark orchid, dc in each of next 2 sts, inc, dc in each of next 3 sts, changing to black, dc in each of next 2 sts, changing to dark orchid, dc in each of next 6 sts, changing to black, dc in each of next 5 sts] 31 times, changing to dark orchid, dc in each of next 2 sts, inc, dc in each of next 3 sts, changing to black, dc in each of next 2 sts, changing to dark orchid, dc in each of next 6 sts, changing to black, join. *(640 sts)*

Rnd 15: Ch 3, dc in each of next 4 sts, [changing to dark orchid, dc in each of next 7 sts, changing to black, dc in each of next 2 sts, changing to dark orchid, dc in each of next 2 sts, inc, dc in each of next 3 sts, changing to black, dc in each of next 5 sts] 31 times, changing to dark orchid, dc in each of next 7 sts, changing to black, dc in each of next 2 sts, changing to dark orchid, dc in each of next 2 sts, inc, dc in each of next 3 sts, changing to black, join in top of ch-3. Fasten off B. *(672 sts)*

Rnd 16: Ch 1, sc in each of first 5 sts, changing to turquoise, pc, [sc in next st, pc] 3 times, changing to black, sc in each of next 2 sts, changing to turquoise, pc, [sc in next st, pc] 3 times, *changing to black, sc in each of next 5 sts, changing to turquoise, pc, [sc in next st, pc] 3 times, changing to black, sc in each of next 2 sts, changing to turquoise, pc, [sc in next st, pc] 3 times, rep from * 30 times, changing to black, join in first sc. Fasten off turquoise.

Rnd 17: Ch 3, dc in each of next 4 sts, [changing to wildflower, sk each ch-1 sp of pc, dc in each of next 7 sts, changing to black, dc in each of next 2 sts, changing to wildflower, dc in each of next 7 sts *, changing to black, dc in each of next 5 sts] 32 times, ending last rep at *, changing to black, join in top of beg ch-3.

Rnds 18–20: Changing colors as established, ch 3, dc in each st around, join. At end of rnd 20, fasten off both colors.

Rnd 21: Sk first 3 black sts and next 7 wildflower sts before black 2-dc group, [for Pyramid, sk next 2 black sts, join wildflower in first wildflower st past black 2-dc group, sc in next st, hdc in next st, dc in each of next 4 sts, changing to black, dc in each of next 5 black sts, changing to wildflower, dc in each of next 4 sts, hdc in next st, sc in next st, sl st in last wildflower st of group, fasten off both colors] 32 times.

Note: Rnds now beg here. (32 Pyramids with 19 sts each)

Rnd 22: [Sk first 4 sts of Pyramid, join wildflower in next st, sc in next st, hdc in next st, changing to black, dc in each of next 5 sts, changing to wildflower, hdc in next st, sc in next st, sl st in next st, leaving last 4 sts unworked, fasten off both colors] in each Pyramid around. *(11 sts in each Pyramid)*

Rnd 23: For Columns *(make 1 in each Pyramid)*, work 7 rows as follows:

A: With WS of work facing, join black with sc in first black dc on Pyramid, sc in each of next 4 sts, leaving rem sts unworked, turn. *(5 sc)*

B: [Ch 1, sc in each st across, turn] 6 times for a total of 7 sc rows. At end of last row, fasten off. On last Column, do not fasten off.

Rnd 24: Ch 1, [sc in each of next 5 sts across top of Column, ch 1, sc in end of each of next 7 rows, sc in each of next 16 unworked sts of rnds 20–22 to next Column, sc in end of next Column, sc in ends of next 7 rows on column, ch 1] 32 times, join in first sc. Fasten off.

Small Heptagon

Make 32.

With wildflower, ch 4, join in first ch to form ring.

Rnd 1: Ch 3, 13 dc in ring, join in top of ch 3. *(14 dc)*

Rnd 2: Ch 4 *(counts as first dc and ch-1 sp)* dc in same st as beg ch-4, dc in next st, dc in next st] 6 times, join in 3rd ch of beg ch-4. *(21 dc, 7 ch-1 sps)*

Rnds 3 & 4: (Sl st, ch 4, dc) in first ch sp, [dc in each st around to next ch-1 sp, (dc, ch 1, dc) in ch-1 sp] 6 times, dc in each st around, join in 3rd ch of beg ch-4. At end of rnd 4, fasten off. *(35 dc, 49 dc)*

Rnd 5: Join black with sc in any ch-1 sp, sc in each st and in each ch sp around, join in first sc. Fasten off. *(56 sc)*

Matching corners, sew Small Heptagons to last rnd of Third Section between Columns *(see Assembly Diagram)*.

FOURTH SECTION

Rnd 1: Working around entire afghan, spacing sts evenly, join black with sc in first st worked into corner of any Column, sc in each of next 4 sts, 7 sc up side of next Small Heptagon, (sc, ch 1, sc) in corner st, 7 sc across top of Small Heptagon, mark 3rd st of last 7 sc made, (sc, ch 1, sc) in next corner st, 7 sc down side of Small Heptagon, [sc in each of next 5 sts across top of Column, 7 sc up side of next Small Heptagon, (sc, ch 1, sc) in corner st, 7 sc across top of Small Heptagon, mark 3rd st of last 7 sc made, (sc, ch 1, sc) in next corner st, 7 sc down side of Small Heptagon] 31 times, join in first sc. Fasten off. *(30 sc in each rep—960 sc, 64 ch-1 sps)*

Rnd 2: For Half Circle, work 3 rows as follows:

A: With dark orchid, join with sc in next marked st, sk next st, (3 dc, ch 1, 3 dc) in next st, sk next st, sc in each of next 2 sts, turn. *(9 sts, 1 ch sp)*

B: 3 dc in 2nd dc of next 3-dc group, ch 1, 3 dc in next ch sp, ch 1, 3 dc in 2nd dc of next 3-dc group, sk next st on rnd 1 of Fourth Section, sc in each of next 3 sts, turn. *(3 dc groups, 2 ch sps)*

C: Work 3 dc in 2nd dc of each 3-dc group and in each ch sp across, sk next st on rnd 1 of Fourth Section, sl st in next st. Fasten off. *(15 dc)*

D: [Rep steps A–C consecutively] 31 times for a total of 32 Half Circles.

Rnd 3: Working on rnd 1, join black in first st of any column, ch 3, *dc in each of next 3 sts, dc dec, sc in each of next 7 sts, working across Half Circle in dc only, sk first st, [sc in each of next 3 sts, 2 sc in next st] 3 times, sc in each of next 3 sts, working on rnd 1, sc in each of next 7 sts **, dc dec, rep from * 31 times, ending last rep at **, sk last st, join in top of ch-3. *(37 sts in each rep—1,184 sts total)*

Rnd 4: Ch 3, [dc in each of next 3 sts, dc dec, hdc in each of next 10 sts, 2 hdc in next st, hdc in each of next 8 sts, 2 hdc in next st, hdc in each of next 10 sts, dc dec] 31 times, dc in each of next 3 sts, dc dec, hdc in each of next 10 sts, 2 hdc in next st, hdc in each of next 8 sts, 2 hdc in next st, hdc in each of next 10 sts, sk last st, join in top of ch-3.

Rnd 5: Ch 3, *dc in each of next 3 sts, dc dec, [dc in each of next 7 sts, inc] 3 times, dc in each of next 6 sts, dc dec, rep from * 30 times, dc in each of next 3 sts, dc dec, [dc in each of next 7 sts, inc] 3 times, dc in each of next 6 sts, sk last st, join in top of ch-3. *(38 sts in each rep—1,216 dc)*

Rnd 6: Sl st in next st, (sl st, ch 1, sc) in next st, sk next 2 sts, 5 dc in next st, sk next 2 sts, sc in next st, sk next 2 sts, 5 dc in next st, [sk next st, sc in next st, sk next st, 5 dc in next st] 5 times, *[sk next 2 sts, sc in next st, sk next 2 sts, 5 dc in next st] 3 times, [sk next st, sc in next st, sk next st, 5 dc in next st] 5 times, rep from * 30 times, sk next 2 sts, sc in next st, sk next 2 sts, 5 dc in next st, sk last st, sk next 2 sl sts, join in first sc. Fasten off. •

HONEY BUNCH BLANKET

This matelassé-style blanket is all about beautifully crocheted textures! Worked in worsted-weight yarn in the round, this stunning baby blanket is sure to become an heirloom.

①②③④⑤⑥ INTERMEDIATE

FINISHED MEASUREMENT

36 inches across

MATERIALS

- Patons Canadiana medium (worsted) weight acrylic yarn (3½ oz/205 yds/100g per ball):
    7 balls #743 pale teal
- Size G/6/4mm crochet hook or size needed to obtain gauge
- Tapestry needle

GAUGE

Rnds 1–9 = 6 inches across

PATTERN NOTES

Patons Canadiana is a soft, pliable, light worsted-weight yarn. Using a heavier, stiffer worsted-weight yarn will result in a thick, heavy, stiff blanket.

You may find some rounds tend to cup or ruffle the piece. This is normal for this pattern. Subsequent rounds will alleviate the cupping or ruffling.

Weave in loose ends as work progresses.

Join with slip stitch as indicated unless otherwise stated.

Chain-3 at beginning of row counts as first double crochet unless otherwise stated.

BLANKET

Ch 4; **join** *(see Pattern Notes)* in the first ch to form a ring.

Rnd 1: Ch 1, work 8 sc in the ring; join in the first sc. *(8 sc)*

Rnd 2: Ch 3 *(see Pattern Notes)*, dc in the same st as joining, (2 dc in the next sc) 7 times; join in the top of the beg ch-3. *(16 dc)*

Rnd 3: Ch 1 loosely, (**fpdc**—*see Stitch Guide*, dc) in the first dc, (fpdc, dc) in each of the rem 15 dc around; join in the top of the first fpdc, ch 1; turn. *(16 fpdc, 16 dc)*

Rnd 4: Sc in the first dc, tr in the **back lp** *(see Stitch Guide)* only of the next fpdc, (sc in the next dc, tr in the back lp only of the next fpdc) 15 times; join in the first sc, ch 1; turn. *(16 tr, 16 sc)*

Rnd 5: Inserting hook in the top of the first tr and into the unworked lp at the base of the same tr, work a sc, ch 1, sc in the next sc, ch 1, *inserting hook in the top of the next tr and into the unworked lp at the base of the same tr, work a sc, ch 1, sc in the next sc, ch 1, rep from * 14 times; join in the first sc, ch 1; turn. *(32 sc, 32 ch-1 sps)*

Rnd 6: Sc in the first ch-1 sp, tr in the back lp only of the next sc, sc in the next ch-1 sp, ch 1, sk next sc, (sc in the next ch-1 sp, tr in the back lp only of the next sc, sc in the next ch-1 sp, ch 1, sk next sc) around; join in the first sc, ch 1; turn. *(16 tr, 32 sc, 16 ch-1 sps)*

Rnd 7: Sc in the first ch-1 sp, ch 1, sk next sc, inserting hook in the top of the next tr and into the unworked lp at the base of the same tr, work a sc, ch 1, sk next sc, (sc in the next ch-1 sp, ch 1, sk next sc, inserting hook in the top of the next tr and into the unworked lp at the base of the same tr, work a sc, ch 1, sk next sc) around; join in the first sc, ch 1; turn. *(32 sc, 32 ch-1 sps)*

Rnd 8: Sc in the first ch-1 sp, ch 1, sk next sc, sc in the next ch-1 sp, tr in the back lp only of the next sc, (sc in the next ch-1 sp, ch 1, sk next sc, sc in the next ch-1 sp, tr in the back lp only of the next sc) around; join in the first sc, ch 1; turn. *(16 tr, 32 sc, 16 ch-1 sps)*

Rnd 9: Inserting hook in the top of the first tr and into the unworked lp at the base of the same tr, work a sc, sk next sc, 5 dc in the next ch-1 sp, sk next sc, (inserting hook in the top of the next tr and into the unworked lp at the base of the same tr, work a sc, sk next sc, 5 dc in the next ch-1 sp, sk next sc) around; join in the first sc. *(16 sc, 16 5-dc groups)*

Rnd 10: Working behind the sts on the previous rnd, ch 1, sc through the 2 **vertical bars on the back of the first sc** *(see illustration)*, ch 4, sk 5 dc, *sc through the 2 vertical bars on the back of the next sc**, ch 4, sk 5 dc, rep from * around, ending last rep at **, sk 5 dc, (ch 1, join with a dc in the first sc) to form the first ch-4 sp for the next rnd. *(16 sc, 16 ch-4 sps)*

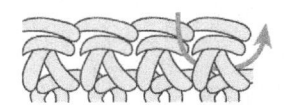

Vertical Strand Sc

Rnd 11: Sl st in the center of the same ch-4 sp, ch 3, (2 dc, sc) in the same ch-4 sp, ch 1, sk next sc, *(sc, 3 dc, sc) in the next ch-4 sp, ch 1, sk next sc, rep from * around, sc in the first ch-4 sp; join in the top of the beg ch-3. *(48 dc, 32 sc, 16 ch-1 sps)*

Rnd 12: Ch 1 loosely, fpdc around the first dc, fpdc around each of the next 2 dc, ch 1, sk next sc, sc in the next ch-1 sp, ch 1, sk next sc, (fpdc around each of the next 3 dc, ch 1, sk next sc, sc in the next ch-1 sp, ch 1, sk next sc) around; join in the top of the first fpdc. *(48 fpdc, 16 sc, 32 ch-1 sps)*

Rnd 13: Ch 1 loosely, fpdc around each of the next 3 fpdc, sc in the next ch-1 sp, ch 1, sk next sc, sc in the next ch-1 sp, (fpdc around each of the next 3 fpdc, sc in the next ch-1 sp, ch 1, sk next sc, sc in the next ch-1 sp) around; join in the top of the first fpdc. *(48 fpdc, 32 sc, 16 ch-1 sps)*

Rnds 14 & 15: Rep rnds 12 and 13.

Rnd 16: Rep rnd 12. *(48 fpdc, 16 sc, 32 ch-1 sps)*

Rnd 17: Ch 1, *fpsc around each of the next 3 fpdc, sc in each of the next (ch-1 sp, sc, ch-1 sp), rep from * around; join in the **front lp** *(see Stitch Guide)* only of the first fpsc. *(48 fpsc, 48 sc)*

Rnd 18: Ch 3, dc in the front lp only of each of the rem sts around; join in the top of the beg ch-3. *(96 sts)*

Rnd 19: Ch 1, inserting hook into the top of the first dc and into the unworked back lp at the base of the same dc, work a sc, (inserting hook into the top of the next dc and into the unworked back lp at the base of the same dc, work a sc) around; join in the first sc.

Rnd 20: Ch 1, sc in the same st as joining, ch 1, (sc in the next sc, ch 1) 95 times; join in the first sc, ch 1; turn. *(96 sc, 96 ch-1 sps)*

Rnd 21: Rep rnd 6. *(48 tr, 96 sc, 48 ch-1 sps)*

Rnd 22: Rep rnd 7. *(96 sc, 96 ch-1 sps)*

Rnd 23: Rep rnd 8. *(48 tr, 96 sc, 48 ch-1 sps)*

Rnd 24: Inserting hook in the top of the first tr and into the unworked lp at the base of the same tr, work a sc, ch 1, sk next sc, sc in the next ch-1 sp, ch 1, sk next sc, (inserting hook in the top of the next tr and into the unworked lp at the base of the same tr, work a sc, ch 1, sk next sc, sc in the next ch-1 sp, ch 1, sk next sc) around; join in the first sc, ch 1; turn. *(96 sc, 96 ch-1 sps)*

Rnds 25–32: [Rep rnds 21–24] twice.

Rnds 33–35: Rep rnds 21–23. *(48 tr, 96 sc, 48 ch-1 sps)*

Rnds 36–40: Rep rnds 9–13. *(144 fpdc, 96 sc, 48 ch-1 sps)*

Rnds 41–44: [Rep rnds 39 and 40] twice.

Rnd 45: Rep rnd 39. *(144 fpdc, 48 sc, 96 ch-1 sps)*

Rnd 46: Rep rnd 17. *(144 fpsc, 144 sc)*

Rnds 47 & 48: Rep rnds 18 and 19. *(288 sts)*

Rnd 49: Ch 1, sc in the same st as joining, *ch 1, sk next sc, sc in the next sc, ch 1**, sc in the next sc, rep from * around, ending last rep at **; join in the first sc, turn. *(192 sc, 192 ch-1 sps)*

Rnds 50–53: Rep rnds 21–24.

Rnds 54–65: [Rep rnds 21–24] 3 times.

Rnds 66–68: Rep rnds 21–23. *(96 tr, 192 sc, 96 ch-1 sps)*

Rnd 69: Rep rnd 9. *(96 sc, 96 5-dc groups)* Fasten off.

RAINBOW STAR BABY BLANKET

Watch this mesmerizing blanket take shape as you crochet from the center out, forming the colorful star design. Pompoms add a fun and playful touch.

①②③④⑤⑥ **EASY**

FINISHED MEASUREMENTS

37⅜ inches from point to point; 253/8 inches smallest width

MATERIALS

3 LIGHT

- Lion Brand Mandala light (DK) weight acrylic yarn (51/3 oz/590 yds/150g per cake):
    1 cake each #205 pixie, #210 Pegasus
- Size 7/4.5mm crochet hook or size needed to obtain gauge
- Tapestry needle
- Stitch marker
- 1¾-inch pompom maker

GAUGE

In Pattern: 17 sts = 4 inches; Rnds 1–7 = 4 inches, after blocking

PATTERN NOTES

Weave in loose ends as work progresses.

Join with slip stitch as indicated unless otherwise stated.

Place marker on first stitch of round and move up as each round is completed.

Chain-3 at beginning of round counts as first double crochet unless otherwise stated.

BLANKET

Rnd 1: With Pegasus, make a **slip ring** *(see illustration)*. **Ch 3** *(see Pattern Notes)*, 11 dc in ring, **join** *(see Pattern Notes)* in top of beg ch-3. **Place marker** *(see Pattern Notes)*. *(12 dc)*

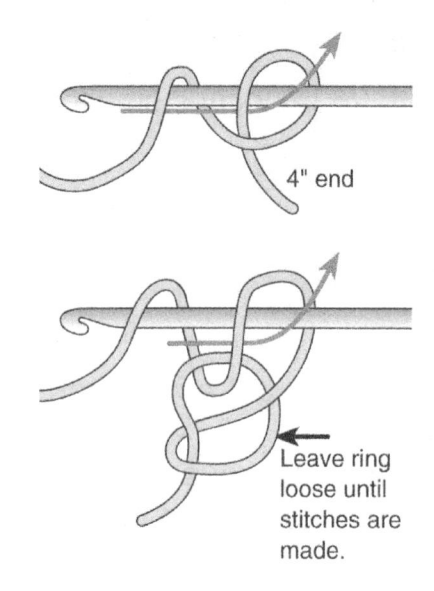

Slip Ring

Rnd 2: Ch 3, 3 dc in next dc, [dc in next dc, 3 dc in next dc] 5 times, join in top of beg ch-3. *(24 dc)*

Rnd 3: Ch 1, sc in first dc, * **fpdc** *(see Stitch Guide)* around next dc, (dc, tr, dc) in next dc, fpdc around next dc**, sc in next dc, rep from * around ending last rep at **, join in first st. *(36 sts)*

Rnd 4: Ch 1, sc in first sc, *fpdc around next fpdc, dc in next dc (dc, tr, dc) in next tr, dc in next dc, fpdc around next fpdc**, sc in next sc, rep from * around ending last rep at **, join in first st. *(48 sts)*

Rnd 5: Ch 1, sc in first sc, *fpdc around next fpdc, dc in next dc, fpdc around next dc, (dc, tr, dc) in next tr, fpdc around next dc, dc in next dc, fpdc around next fpdc**, sc in next sc, rep from * around ending last rep at **, join in first st. *(60 sts)*

Rnd 6: Ch 1, sc in first sc, *[fpdc around next st, dc in next dc] twice, (dc, tr, dc) in next tr, [dc in next dc, fpdc around next st] twice**, sc in next sc, rep from * around ending last rep at **, join in first st. *(72 sts)*

Rnd 7: Ch 1, sc in first sc, *[fpdc around next fpdc, dc in next dc] twice, fpdc around next dc, (dc, tr, dc) in next tr, fpdc around next dc, [dc in next dc, fpdc around next fpdc] twice**, sc in next sc, rep from * around ending last rep at **, join in first st. *(84 sts)*

Rnd 8: Ch 1, sc in first sc, *[fpdc around next fpdc, dc in next dc] across to next tr, (dc, tr, dc) in next tr, [dc in next dc, fpdc around next fpdc] across to next sc**, sc in next sc, rep from * around ending last rep at **, join in first st. *(96 sts)*

Rnd 9: Ch 1, sc in first sc, *[fpdc around next fpdc, dc in next dc] across to last dc before next tr, fpdc around next dc, (dc, tr, dc) in next tr, fpdc around next dc, [dc in next dc, fpdc around next fpdc] across to next sc**, sc in next sc, rep from * around ending last rep at **, join in first st. *(108 sts)*

Rnds 10–40: [Rep rnds 8 and 9] 15 times, rep rnd 8 once more. Change to pixie when Pegasus cake is finished. *(480 sts)*

Fasten off.

FINISHING

Block the blanket.

Make 6 pompoms and sew to the tr on each tip of the star.

Weave in all ends.

ALEGRIA AFGHAN

Stunning textures meet gorgeous colors! Crocheted in the round using self-striping worsted-weight yarn and a variety of post stitches, you'll find this project hard to put down!

INTERMEDIATE

FINISHED MEASUREMENT

58 inches in diameter

MATERIALS

- Red Heart Super Saver Stripes medium (worsted) weight acrylic yarn (5 oz/236 yds/141g per skein):
    15 skeins #4961 preppy stripe
- Size H/8/5mm crochet hook or size needed to obtain gauge
- Tapestry needle

GAUGE

Rnds 1–6 = 5¼ inches in diameter

PATTERN NOTES

Weave in loose ends as work progresses.

It's normal for some rounds to cup or ruffle Afghan. Subsequent rounds will alleviate cupping or ruffling.

Join with slip stitch as indicated unless otherwise stated.

Chain-3 at beginning of round counts as first double crochet unless otherwise stated.

Chain-1 loosely at beginning of round does not count as a stitch.

SPECIAL STITCH

Front post double crochet decrease (fpdc dec): Yo, insert hook around both of next 2 fpdc, yo, draw up a lp, [yo, draw through 2 lps on hook] twice.

AFGHAN

Rnd 1 (RS): Ch 6, **join** *(see Pattern Notes)* in first ch of ch-6 to form a ring, **ch 3** *(see Pattern Notes)*, 15 dc in ring, join in 3rd ch of beg ch-3. *(16 dc)*

Rnd 2: Ch 1 loosely *(see Pattern Notes)*, **fpdc** *(see Stitch Guide)* around each of first 2 dc, ch 1, [fpdc around each of next 2 dc, ch 1] 7 times, join in top of first fpdc. *(16 fpdc, 8 ch-1 sps)*

Rnd 3: Ch 1 loosely, fpdc around each of first 2 fpdc, ch 1, sc in next ch-1 sp, ch 1, [fpdc around each of next 2 fpdc, ch 1, sc in next ch-1 sp, ch 1] 7 times, join in top of first fpdc. *(16 fpdc, 16 ch-1 sps, 8 sc)*

Rnd 4: Ch 1 loosely, fpdc around each of first 2 fpdc, [ch 1, sc in next ch-1 sp] twice, ch 1, *fpdc around each of next 2 fpdc, [ch 1, sc in next ch-1 sp] twice, ch 1, rep from * around, join in top of first fpdc. *(16 fpdc, 24 ch-1 sps, 16 sc)*

Rnd 5: Ch 1 loosely, fpdc around each of first 2 fpdc, [ch 1, sc in next ch-1 sp] 3 times, ch 1, *fpdc around each of next 2 fpdc, [ch 1, sc in next ch-1 sp] 3 times, ch 1, rep from * around, join in top of first fpdc. *(16 fpdc, 32 ch-1 sps, 24 sc)*

Rnd 6: Ch 1 loosely, fpdc around each of first 2 fpdc, [ch 1, sc in next ch-1 sp] 4 times, ch 1, *fpdc around each of next 2 fpdc, [ch 1, sc in next ch-1 sp] 4 times, ch 1, rep from * around, join top of first fpdc. *(16 fpdc, 40 ch-1 sps, 32 sc)*

Rnd 7: Ch 1 loosely, (fpdc, dc) in first fpdc, (dc, fpdc) in next fpdc, sc in next ch-1 sp, [ch 1, sc in next ch-1 sp] 4 times, *(fpdc, dc) in next fpdc, (dc, fpdc) in next fpdc, sc in next ch-1 sp, [ch 1, sc in next ch-1 sp] 4 times, rep from * around, join in top of first fpdc. *(16 fpdc, 16 dc, 32 ch-1 sps, 40 sc)*

Rnd 8: Ch 1 loosely, fpdc around first fpdc, fpdc around next dc, ch 1, fpdc around next dc, fpdc around next fpdc, sc in next ch-1 sp, [ch 1, sc in next ch-1 sp] 3 times, *fpdc around next fpdc, fpdc around next dc, ch 1, fpdc around next dc, fpdc around next fpdc, sc in next ch-1 sp, [ch 1, sc in next ch-1 sp] 3 times, rep from * around, join in top of first fpdc. *(32 fpdc, 32 ch-1 sps, 32 sc)*

Rnd 9: Ch 1 loosely, fpdc around each of first 2 fpdc, ch 1, sc in next ch-1 sp, ch 1, fpdc around each of next 2 fpdc, sc in next ch-1 sp, [ch 1, sc in next ch-1 sp] twice, *fpdc around each of next 2 fpdc, ch 1, sc in next ch-1 sp, ch 1, fpdc around each of next 2 fpdc, sc in next ch-1 sp, [ch 1, sc in next ch-1 sp] twice, rep from * around, join in top of first fpdc. *(32 fpdc, 32 ch-1 sps, 32 sc)*

Rnd 10: Ch 1 loosely, fpdc around each of first 2 fpdc, [ch 1, sc in next ch-1 sp] twice, ch 1, fpdc around each of next 2 fpdc, sc in next ch-1 sp, ch 1, sc in next ch-1 sp, *fpdc around each of next 2 fpdc, [ch 1, sc in next ch-1 sp] twice, ch 1, fpdc around each of next 2 fpdc, sc in next ch-1 sp, ch 1, sc in next ch-1 sp, rep from * around, join in top of first fpdc. *(32 fpdc, 32 ch-1 sps, 32 sc)*

Rnd 11: Ch 1 loosely, fpdc around each of first 2 fpdc, [ch 1, sc in next ch-1 sp] 3 times, ch 1, fpdc around each of next 2 fpdc, sc in next ch-1 sp, *fpdc around each of next 2 fpdc, [ch 1, sc in next ch-1 sp] 3 times, ch 1, fpdc around each of next 2 fpdc, sc in next ch-1 sp, rep from * around, join in top of first fpdc. *(32 fpdc, 32 ch-1 sps, 32 sc)*

Rnd 12: Ch 1 loosely, fpdc around each of first 2 fpdc, [ch 1, sc in next ch-1 sp] 4 times, ch 1, fpdc around each of next 2 fpdc, sk next sc, *fpdc around each of next 2 fpdc, [ch 1, sc in next ch-1 sp] 4 times, ch 1, fpdc around each of next 2 fpdc, sk next sc, rep from * around, join in top of first fpdc. *(32 fpdc, 40 ch-1 sps, 32 sc)*

Rnd 13: Ch 1 loosely, **fpdc dec** *(see Special Stitch)* around first 2 fpdc, [ch 1, sc in next ch-1 sp] 5 times, ch 1, fpdc dec around next 2 fpdc, *fpdc dec around next 2 fpdc, [ch 1, sc in next ch-1 sp] 5 times, ch 1, fpdc dec around next 2 fpdc, rep from * around, join in top of first fpdc dec. *(16 fpdc dec, 48 ch-1 sps, 40 sc)*

Rnd 14: Ch 1 loosely, fpdc around first fpdc dec, [2 dc in next ch-1 sp, 2 dc in next sc] 5 times, 2 dc in next ch-1 sp, fpdc around next fpdc dec, *fpdc around next fpdc dec, [2 dc in next ch-1 sp, 2 dc in next sc] 5 times, 2 dc in next ch-1 sp, fpdc around next fpdc dec, rep from * around, join in top of first fpdc. *(16 fpdc, 176 dc)*

Rnd 15: Ch 1 loosely, fpdc around first fpdc, [**bpdc** *(see Stitch Guide)* around each of next 2 dc, fpdc around each of the next 2 dc] 5 times, bpdc around each of next 2 dc, fpdc around next fpdc, *fpdc around next fpdc, [bpdc around each of next 2 dc, fpdc around each of next 2 dc] 5 times, bpdc around each of next 2 dc, fpdc around next fpdc, rep from * around, join in top of first fpdc. *(96 fpdc, 96 bpdc)*

Rnds 16–26: Ch 1 loosely, fpdc around first fpdc, [bpdc around each of next 2 bpdc, fpdc around each of next 2 fpdc] 47 times, bpdc around each of next 2 bpdc, fpdc around next fpdc, join in top of first fpdc. *(96 fpdc, 96 bpdc)*

Rnd 27: Ch 1 loosely, fpdc around first fpdc, sc in next bpdc, [ch 1, sc in next st] 9 times, fpdc in next fpdc, *fpdc in next fpdc, sc in next bpdc, [ch 1, sc in next st] 9 times, fpdc around next fpdc, rep from * around, join in top of first fpdc. *(32 fpdc, 144 ch-1 sps, 160 sc)*

Rnd 28: Ch 3, fpdc around first fpdc, sc in next ch-1 sp, [ch 1, sc in next ch-1 sp] 8 times, (fpdc, dc) in next fpdc, *(dc, fpdc) in next fpdc, sc in next ch-1 sp, [ch 1, sc in next ch-1 sp] 8 times, (fpdc, dc) in next fpdc, rep from * around, join in top of beg ch-3. *(32 fpdc, 32 dc, 112 ch-1 sps, 144 sc)*

Rnd 29: Ch 1 loosely, fpdc around first dc, fpdc around next fpdc, sc in next ch-1 sp, [ch 1, sc in next sc] 7 times, fpdc around next fpdc, fpdc around next dc, ch 1, *fpdc around next dc, fpdc around next fpdc, sc in next ch-1 sp, [ch 1, sc in next ch-1 sp] 7 times, fpdc around next fpdc, fpdc around next dc, ch 1, rep from * around, join in top of first fpdc. *(64 fpdc, 128 ch-1 sps, 128 sc)*

Rnd 30: Ch 1 loosely, fpdc around each of first 2 fpdc, sc in next ch-1 sp, [ch 1, sc in next ch-1 sp] 6 times, fpdc around each of next 2 fpdc, ch 1, sc in next ch-1 sp, ch 1, *fpdc around each of next 2 fpdc, sc in next ch-1 sp, [ch 1, sc in next ch-1 sp] 6 times, fpdc around each of next 2 fpdc, ch 1, sc in next ch-1 sp, ch 1, rep from * around, join in top of first fpdc. *(64 fpdc, 128 ch-1 sps, 128 sc)*

Rnd 31: Ch 1 loosely, fpdc around each of first 2 fpdc, sc in next ch-1 sp, [ch 1, sc in next ch-1 sp] 5 times, fpdc around each of next 2 fpdc, [ch 1, sc in next ch-1 sp] 2 times, ch 1, *fpdc around each of next 2 fpdc, sc in next ch-1 sp, [ch 1, sc in next ch-1 sp] 5 times, fpdc around each of next 2 fpdc, [ch 1, sc in next ch-1 sp] 2 times, ch 1, rep from * around, join in top of first fpdc. *(64 fpdc, 128 ch-1 sps, 128 sc)*

Rnd 32: Ch 1 loosely, fpdc around each of first 2 fpdc, sc in next ch-1 sp, [ch 1, sc in next ch-1 sp] 4 times, fpdc around each of next 2 fpdc, [ch 1, sc in next ch-1 sp] 3 times, ch 1, *fpdc around each of next 2 fpdc, sc in next ch-1 sp, [ch 1, sc in next ch-1 sp] 4 times, fpdc around each of next 2 fpdc, [ch 1, sc in next ch-1 sp] 3 times, ch 1, rep from * around, join in top of first fpdc. *(64 fpdc, 128 ch-1 sps, 128 sc)*

Rnd 33: Ch 1 loosely, fpdc around each of first 2 fpdc, sc in next ch-1 sp, [ch 1, sc in next ch-1 sp] 3 times, fpdc around each of next 2 fpdc, [ch 1, sc in next ch-1 sp] 4 times, ch 1, *fpdc around each of next 2 fpdc, sc in next ch-1 sp, [ch 1, sc in next ch-1 sp] 3 times, fpdc around each of next 2 fpdc, [ch 1, sc in next ch-1 sp] 4 times, ch 1, rep from * around, join in top of first fpdc. *(64 fpdc, 128 ch-1 sps, 128 sc)*

Rnd 34: Ch 1 loosely, fpdc around each of first 2 fpdc, sc in next ch-1 sp, [ch 1, sc in next ch-1 sp] twice, fpdc around each of next 2 fpdc, [ch 1, sc in next ch-1 sp] 5 times, ch 1, *fpdc around each of next 2 fpdc, sc in next ch-1 sp, [ch 1, sc in next ch-1 sp] twice, fpdc around each of next 2 fpdc, [ch 1, sc in next ch-1 sp] 5 times, ch 1, rep from * around, join in top of first fpdc. *(64 fpdc, 128 ch-1 sps, 128 sc)*

Rnd 35: Ch 1 loosely, fpdc around each of first 2 fpdc, sc in next ch-1 sp, ch 1, sc in next ch-1 sp, fpdc around each of next 2 fpdc, [ch 1, sc in next ch-1 sp] 6 times, ch 1, *fpdc around each of next 2 fpdc, sc in next ch-1 sp, ch 1, sc in next ch-1 sp, fpdc around each of next 2 fpdc, [ch 1, sc in next ch-1 sp] 6 times, ch 1, rep from * around, join in top of first fpdc. *(64 fpdc, 128 ch-1 sps, 128 sc)*

Rnd 36: Ch 1 loosely, fpdc around each of first 2 fpdc, ch 1, sc in next ch-1 sp, ch 1, fpdc around each of next 2 fpdc, sc in next ch-1 sp, [ch 1, sc in next ch-1 sp] 6 times, *fpdc around each of next 2 fpdc, ch 1, sc in next ch-1 sp, ch 1, fpdc in each of next 2 fpdc, sc in next ch-1 sp, [ch 1, sc in next ch-1 sp] 6 times, rep from * around, join in top of first fpdc. *(64 fpdc, 128 ch-1 sps, 128 sc)*

Rnd 37: Ch 1 loosely, fpdc around each of first 2 fpdc, [ch 1, sc in next ch-1 sp] twice, ch 1, fpdc around each of next 2 fpdc, sc in next ch-1 sp, [ch 1, sc in next ch-1 sp] 5 times, *fpdc around each of next 2 fpdc, [ch 1, sc in next ch-1 sp] twice, ch 1, fpdc around each of next 2 fpdc, sc in next ch-1 sp, [ch 1, sc in next ch-1 sp] 5 times, rep from * around, join in top of first fpdc. *(64 fpdc, 128 ch-1 sps, 128 sc)*

Rnd 38: Ch 1 loosely, fpdc around each of first 2 fpdc, [ch 1, sc in next ch-1 sp] 3 times, ch 1, fpdc around each of next 2 fpdc, sc in next ch-1 sp, [ch 1, sc in next ch-1 sp] 4 times, *fpdc around each of next 2 fpdc, [ch 1, sc in next ch-1 sp] 3 times, ch 1, fpdc around each of next 2 fpdc, sc in next ch-1 sp, [ch 1, sc in next ch-1 sp] 4 times, rep from * around, join in top of first fpdc. *(64 fpdc, 128 ch-1 sps, 128 sc)*

Rnd 39: Ch 1 loosely, fpdc around each of first 2 fpdc, [ch 1, sc in next ch-1 sp] 4 times, ch 1, fpdc around each of next 2 fpdc, sc in next ch-1 sp, [ch 1, sc in next ch-1 sp] 3 times, *fpdc around each of next 2 fpdc, [ch 1, sc in next ch-1 sp] 4 times, ch 1, fpdc around each of next 2 fpdc, sc in next ch-1 sp, [ch 1, sc in next ch-1 sp] 3 times, rep from * around, join in top of first fpdc. *(64 fpdc, 128 ch-1 sps, 128 sc)*

Rnd 40: Ch 1 loosely, fpdc around each of first 2 fpdc, [ch 1, sc in next ch-1 sp] 5 times, ch 1, fpdc in each of next 2 fpdc, sc in next ch-1 sp, [ch 1, sc in next ch-1 sp] twice, *fpdc around each of next 2 fpdc, [ch 1, sc in next ch-1 sp] 5 times, ch 1, fpdc around each of next 2 fpdc, sc in next ch-1 sp, [ch 1, sc in next ch-1 sp] twice, rep from * around, join in top of first fpdc. *(64 fpdc, 128 ch-1 sps, 128 sc)*

Rnd 41: Ch 1 loosely, fpdc around each of first 2 fpdc, [ch 1, sc in next ch-1 sp] 6 times, ch 1, fpdc in each of next 2 fpdc, sc in next ch-1 sp, ch 1, sc in next ch-1 sp, *fpdc around each of next 2 fpdc, [ch 1, sc in next ch-1 sp] 6 times, ch 1, fpdc around each of next 2 fpdc, sc in next ch-1 sp, ch 1, sc in next ch-1 sp, rep from * around, join in top of first fpdc. *(64 fpdc, 128 ch-1 sps, 128 sc)*

Rnd 42: Ch 1 loosely, fpdc around each of first 2 fpdc, [ch 1, sc in next ch-1 sp] 7 times, ch 1, fpdc around each of next 2 fpdc, sc in next ch-1 sp, *fpdc around each of next 2 fpdc, [ch 1, sc in next ch-1 sp] 7 times, ch 1, fpdc around each of next 2 fpdc, sc in next ch-1 sp, rep from * around, join in top of first fpdc. *(64 fpdc, 128 ch-1 sps, 128 sc)*

Rnd 43: Ch 1 loosely, fpdc around each of first 2 fpdc, [ch 1, sc in next ch-1 sp] 8 times, ch 1, fpdc around each of next 2 fpdc, sk next sc, *fpdc around each of next 2 fpdc, [ch 1, sc in next ch-1 sp] 8 times, ch 1, fpdc around each of next 2 fpdc, sk next sc, rep from * around, join in top of first fpdc. *(64 fpdc, 144 ch-1 sps, 128 sc)*

Rnd 44: Ch 1 loosely, fpdc dec over first 2 fpdc, [ch 1, sc in next ch-1 sp] 9 times, ch 1, fpdc dec over the next 2 fpdc, *fpdc dec over next 2 fpdc, [ch 1, sc in next ch-1 sp] 9 times, ch 1, fpdc dec over next 2 fpdc, rep from * around, join in top of first fpdc dec. *(32 fpdc dec, 160 ch-1 sps, 144 sc)*

Rnd 45: Ch 1 loosely, fpdc around first fpdc dec, [2 dc in next ch-1 sp, dc in next sc] 4 times, 2 dc in next ch-1 sp, 2 dc in next sc, 2 dc in next ch-1 sp, [dc in next sc, 2 dc in next ch-1 sp] 4 times *(total 30 dc)*, fpdc around next fpdc dec, *fpdc around next fpdc dec, [2 dc in next ch-1 sp, dc in next sc] 4 times, 2 dc in next ch-1 sp, 2 dc in next sc, 2 dc in next ch-1 sp, [dc in next sc, 2 dc in next ch-1 sp] 4 times *(total 30 dc)*, fpdc around next fpdc dec, rep from * around, join in top of first fpdc. *(32 fpdc, 480 dc)*

Rnd 46: Ch 1 loosely, fpdc around first fpdc, [bpdc around each of next 2 dc, fpdc around each of next 2 dc] 7 times, bpdc around each of next 2 dc, fpdc around next fpdc, *fpdc in next fpdc, [bpdc around each of next 2 dc, fpdc around each of next 2 dc] 7 times, bpdc around each of next 2 dc, fpdc around next fpdc, rep from * around, join in top of first fpdc. *(256 fpdc, 256 bpdc)*

Rnds 47–59: Ch 1 loosely, fpdc around first fpdc, [bpdc around each of next 2 bpdc, fpdc around each of next 2 fpdc] 127 times, bpdc around each of next 2 bpdc, fpdc in next fpdc, join in top of first fpdc. *(256 fpdc, 256 bpdc)*

Rnd 60: Ch 1 loosely, fpdc around first fpdc, sc in next bpdc, ch 1, sk next bpdc, sc in next fpdc, ch 1, sc in next fpdc, ch 1, sk next bpdc, sc in next bpdc, [ch 1, sc in next fpdc] twice, ch 1, sc in next bpdc, ch 1, sk next bpdc, sc in next fpdc, ch 1, sc in next fpdc, ch 1, sk next bpdc, sc in next bpdc, fpdc around next fpdc, *fpdc around next fpdc, sc in next bpdc, ch 1, sk next bpdc, sc in next fpdc, ch 1, sc in next fpdc, ch 1, sk next bpdc, sc in next bpdc, [ch 1, sc in next fpdc] twice, ch 1, sc in next bpdc, ch 1, sk next bpdc, sc in next fpdc, ch 1, sc in next fpdc, ch 1, sk next bpdc, sc in next bpdc, fpdc around next fpdc, rep from * around, join in top of first fpdc. *(64 fpdc, 288 ch-1 sps, 300 sc)*

Rnds 61–77: Rep rnds 28–44. When working rnds 61–77 the st count will double at the end of each rnd. *(64 fpdc dec, 320 ch-1 sps, 288 sc after rnd 77)*

Rnd 78: Ch 1 loosely, fpdc around first fpdc dec, [dc in next ch-1 sp, dc in next sc] 9 times, dc in next ch-1 sp, fpdc around next fpdc dec, *fpdc around next fpdc dec, [dc in next ch-1 sp, dc in next sc] 9 times, dc in next ch-1 sp, fpdc around next fpdc dec, rep from * around, join in top of first fpdc. *(64 fpdc, 608 dc)*

Rnd 79: Ch 1 loosely, bpdc around first fpdc, bpdc around each of next 19 dc, bpdc around next fpdc, *bpdc around next fpdc, bpdc around each of next 19 dc, bpdc around next fpdc, rep from * around, join in top of first bpdc. *(672 bpdc)*

Rnds 80–83: Ch 1 loosely, bpdc around first bpdc, bpdc around each rem bpdc around, join in top of first bpdc. *(672 bpdc)*

Rnd 84: Sl st in each bpdc around, join in first sl st to keep edge from curling. Fasten off. *(672 sl sts)*

ELLIE ROO

Starting at the center with a simple flower motif, watch this mandala afghan grow round by round. Alternating rounds of textured and lacy stitches add to the beauty.

①②③④⑤⑥ **INTERMEDIATE**

FINISHED MEASUREMENTS
51 inches × 53½ inches

MATERIALS

- Lion Brand Mandala light (DK) weight acrylic yarn (5¼ oz/590 yds/150g per cake):
    3 cakes each #225 sprite (A) and #233 kraken (B)
- Size H/8/5mm crochet hook or size needed to obtain gauge
- Stitch marker
- Tapestry needle

GAUGE
16 sts = 4 inches; 9 pattern rows = 4 inches

PATTERN NOTES
Pattern is written in 4 sections:

Section 1: Center Square.

Section 2: 9-Round Repeat.

Section 3: Border A.

Section 4: Border B.

Pattern is written for a 2-color combo—color A and color B—but is not limited to the color sequence.

Chains at the beginning of a round do not count as stitches.

To avoid cutting your yarn for each color change, attach a stitch marker to the color not being used and keep the loop in the back of your work. Your starting chains will range between 3–7 stitches. You'll want them to come up to the current round or just above.

In round 6 you'll leave chain-4 stitches unworked.

In round 8 you'll turn your work into an octagon.

In round 10 you'll turn your work into a square.

In round 10 the slip stitch counts as a stitch.

Repeat Section 2 five times. To continue increasing add the following numbers to your rounds to keep your stitch count correct:

Round 1: Add 12 bean sts.

Round 2: Add 12 bean sts.

Round 3: Add 23 sc.

Round 4: Add 23 sc.

Round 5: Add 14 dc.

Round 6: Add 5-dc fan.

Round 7: Add 16 dc.

Round 8: Add 24 hdc.

Round 9: Add 24 hdc.

Change colors every 2 rounds for the border.

You can repeat Border A as many times as you want, adding 1 half double crochet per corner for stitch count.

You can repeat Border B as many times as you want.

Join with slip stitch as indicated unless otherwise stated.

SPECIAL STITCHES

5-double crochet fan (5-dc fan): 5 dc into the same st.

Extended double crochet (ext dc): Yo, insert hook into st, pull up a lp, pull through 1 lp, yo, pull through 2 lps, yo, pull through 2 lps.

Extended double crochet corner (ext dc corner): (Ext dc, ch 3, ext dc) in corner.

Bean stitch (bean st): All sts are in the same st. Insert hook in st, yo, pull up lp *(2 lps on hook)*, yo, insert hook, pull up lp *(4 lps on hook)*. Yo, insert hook, pull up lp *(6 lps on hook)*. Yo, pull through all lps, ch-1.

Corner bean stitch (corner bean st): (Bean st, ch 3, bean st) in corner sp.

BLANKET

SECTION 1

Center Square

Rnd 1: With color A, ch 4, **join** *(see Pattern Notes)* in first ch to form ring, 12 dc in ring, join to first dc. *(12 dc)*

Rnd 2: Ch 2 *(see Pattern Notes)*, 2 dc into each dc around, join to first dc. *(24 dc)*

Rnd 3: Ch 2, [dc in next st, 2 dc in next st] around, join to first dc. *(36 dc)*

Rnd 4: Ch 2, sk first st, [**5-dc fan** *(see Special Stitches)* in next st, sk next 2 dc] around, join to first dc. **Change color** *(see Pattern Notes)* to B. *(12 5-dc fans)*

Rnd 5: Ch 1, [working in the sp between sk 2 dc from rnd 3 and over the st from rnd 4, sc in next st, ch 4, sk 5-dc fan] around, join to first sc. Push the 5-dc fan to the front of the ch, leaving the ch-4 behind your work and unused. *(12 sc, 48 chs)*

Rnd 6: Ch 2, dc in sc, ch 1, [sk first dc, **bpdc** *(see Stitch Guide)* around each of next 3 dc, sk last dc, ch 1, dc in sc, ch 1] 11 times, sk first dc, bpdc around each of next 3 dc, sk the last dc, ch 1, join to first dc. Change colors. *(12 dc, 36 bpdc, 24 ch-1 sps)*

Rnd 7: Ch-5, hdc in each dc, and in each ch-1 sp around, join to first hdc. Change colors. *(72 hdc)*

Rnd 8: *(See Pattern Notes)*, ch 2, [(hdc, ch 2, hdc) in same sp *(corner)*, hdc in next 8 sts] 8 times. *(64 hdc, 8 corners)*

Rnd 9: Sl st to corner sp, ch-1, [sc in **back lp** *(see Stitch Guide)* across with 3 sc in ch-2 sp] 8 times, join to first sc. Change colors. *(80 sc, 8 3-sc corners)*

Rnd 10: *(See Pattern Notes)*, ch-5, start in the center sc in the closest corner sp, [(**ext dc**—*see Special Stitches*, ch 2, ext dc) in same st, ext dc in each of next 3 sts, dc in each of next 3 sts, hdc in each of next 3 sts, sc in each of next 3 sts, **sl st** *(see Pattern Notes)* in next st, sc in each of next 3 sts, hdc in each of next 3 sts, dc in each of next 3 sts, ext dc in each of next 3 sts] 4 times, join to first ext dc. *[6 ext dc, 6 dc, 6 hdc, 6 sc, 1 (sl st, ext dc, ch-2, hdc) group on each side]*

Rnd 11: Sl st to corner sp, ch 1, [3 sc in ch-2 sp, sc in back lp across] 4 times, join to the first sc. Change colors. *(27 sc, 3 sc on each side)*

Rnd 12: Ch 5, [**corner bean st** *(see Special Stitches)* in center corner st, sk sc, {**bean st** *(see Special Stitches)*, sk sc} 14 times] 4 times, join to top of first bean st. *(14 bean sts, 1 corner bean st on each side)*

Rnd 13: Turn work so you are working on the WS, sl st to corner, ch 2, [corner bean st in ch-2 sp, work bean st between each of the bean sts across to the next ch-2 sp] 4 times, join to top of first bean st. Change colors. *(15 bean sts, 1 corner bean st on each side)*

Rnd 14: Turn work to RS, ch 5, [3 sc in the corner sp, sk first st, sc in the top of and in between each bean st] 4 times, join to first sc. *(33 sc with 3 sc in corner on each side)*

Rnd 15: Sl st to corner, ch 1, [3 sc in corner sc, sc in back lp of next 35 sts] 4 times, join to first sc. Change colors. *(35 sc with 3 sc in corner on each side)*

Rnd 16: Ch 5, [(2 dc, ch 2, 2 dc) in corner sc, ch 1, sk 1 st, (dc in next 2 sts, ch 1, sk next st) 12 times] 4 times, join to first dc. *[24 dc, 13 ch-1 sps with (dc, ch 2, dc) in corner on each side]*

Rnd 17: Sl st to corner sp, ch 2, [11 dc in corner sp, (sc in next ch-1 sp, 5-dc fan in next ch-1 sp) 6 times, sc in ch-1 sp] 4 times, join to first dc. Change colors. *(7 sc, 6 5-dc fans with 11 dc in corner on each side)*

SECTION 2

9-Rnd Rep *(See Pattern Notes)*

Rnd 1: Ch 4, [(2 dc, ch 2, 2 dc) into 6th dc of corner, ch 1, sk next dc, (bpdc around each of next 3 dc, ch 1, sk next dc, dc in sc, ch 1, sk next dc) across to the 11 dc corner, bpdc around each of next 3 dc, ch 1, sk next dc] 4 times, join to the first dc. Change colors. *[31 dc, 16 ch-1 sps with (2 dc, ch 2, 2 dc) in corner on each side]*

Rnd 2: Ch 5, [(hdc, ch 2, hdc) in corner sp, hdc in each ch-1 sp and dc across] 4 times, join in first hdc. *[51 hdc with (hdc, ch-2, hdc) in corner on each side]*

Rnd 3: Sl st to corner sp, ch 2 [(hdc, ch-2, hdc) in corner sp, hdc in **back bar** *(see illustration)* across] 4 times, join to first hdc. Change colors. *[53 hdc, 1 (hdc, ch-2, hdc) on each side]*

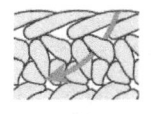

Bar

Rnd 4: Ch 5, [corner bean st, sk hdc, (bean st, sk hdc) 27 times] 4 times, join to top of first bean st. *(27 bean sts with corner bean st in corner on each side)*

Rnd 5: Turn work so you are working on WS, sl st to corner sp, ch 2, [corner bean st in the ch-2 sp, work bean st between each bean st across to next ch-2 sp] 4 times, sl st to top of first bean st. Change colors. *(28 bean sts with corner bean st in corner on each side)*

Rnd 6: Turn work to RS, ch 5, [3 sc in the corner sp, sc in the top of and in between each bean st] 4 times, join to first sc. *(59 sc with 3 sc in corner on each side)*

Rnd 7: Sl st to corner sp, ch 1, [3 sc in corner sc, sc in back lps of next 61 sts] 4 times, join to first sc. Change colors. *(61 sc with 3 sc in corner on each side)*

Rnd 8: Ch 5, [(dc, ch 2, dc) in corner sc, dc in next st, ch 1, sk sc, (dc in next 2 sts, ch 1, sk sc) 20 times, dc in next st] 4 times, join to first dc. *[42 dc, 21 ch-1* *sps with (dc, ch-2, dc) in corner on each side]*

Rnd 9: Sl st to corner sp, ch 2, [11 dc into corner sp, (sc in ch-1 sp, 5-dc fan in ch-1 sp) 10 times, sc in ch-1 sp] 3 times, 11 dc in corner, sc in ch-1 sp, (5-dc fan in ch-1 sp, sc in ch-1 sp) across to first set of dc. join to first dc. Change colors. *(11 sc, 50 dc with 11 dc in corner on each side)*

[Rep rnds 1–9 consecutively] 5 times.

BORDER A *(SEE PATTERN NOTES)*

Rnd 1: Ch 5, [(hdc, ch 2, hdc) in 6th dc on corner, hdc in next 4 sts, sk 1 st, (5-dc fan in sc, sk 2 dc, sc in dc, sk 2 dc) across, 5-dc fan in last sc, sk 1 dc, hdc in the next 4 sts] 4 times, join to first hdc.

Rnd 2: Sl st to corner, ch 1, [(hdc, ch 2, hdc) in corner sp, hdc in back bar in the next 5 sts, (sk 2 dc, sc in next st, sk 2 dc, 5-dc fan in next st) across, sk 2 sts, sc in last fan, sk 2 dc, hdc in the back bar in next 5 sts] 4 times. join to first hdc. Change colors.

[Rep rnds 1 and 2 alternately] **4 times** *(see Pattern Notes)*.

BORDER B

Rnd 1: Ch 5, [(2 dc, ch 2, 2 dc) in corner sp, dc in the next 10 sts, (dc in sc, hdc in next st, sc in next 3 sts, hdc in next st) across, dc in sc, dc in the next 10 sts] 4 times, join to first dc.

Rnd 2: Sl st to corner sp, ch 1, [(hdc, ch 2, hdc) in corner sp, hdc in each st across] 4 times, join to first hdc. Change colors.

Rnd 3: Ch 5, [(hdc, ch 2, hdc) in corner sp, hdc in back bar in each st across] 4 times, join to first hdc.

Rep rnd 3 until desired size and alternating colors every 2 rnds. At end of last rnd, fasten off.

Weave in ends.

DAYSTAR THROW

This throw is crocheted with self-striping yarn so you never have to change colors! Once you set up the stitch repeats, all you need to do is enjoy the rhythmic stitching—the post stitches and chevron peaks make this pattern visually easy to follow.

①②③❹⑤⑥ **INTERMEDIATE**

FINISHED MEASUREMENT
55 inches across

MATERIALS

3 LIGHT

- Lion Brand Yarns Mandala light (DK) weight acrylic yarn (5¼ oz/590 yds/150g per ball):
    4 balls #204 chimera
- Size H/8/5mm crochet hook or size needed to obtain gauge
- Tapestry needle

GAUGE
Rnds 1–3 = 3 inches

PATTERN NOTES
Chain-2 at beginning of round does not count as a stitch unless otherwise stated.

Chain-3 at beginning of round counts as first double crochet unless otherwise stated.

Weave in ends as work progresses.

Join with slip stitch unless otherwise stated.

SPECIAL STITCHES
Beginning V-stitch (beg V-st): Ch 6 *(counts as first dc and ch-3)*, dc in same sp as beg ch-6.

V-stitch (V-st): (Dc, ch 3, dc) in indicated sp.

Beginning popcorn (beg pc): Ch 3, dc 4 times in indicated st, drop lp from hook, insert hook from front to back through top of beg ch-3, place dropped lp on hook and pull through st, ch 1 to close.

Popcorn (pc): Dc 5 times in indicated st, drop lp from hook, insert hook from front to back through top of first st made, place dropped lp on hook and pull through st, ch 1 to close.

THROW

Rnd 1 (RS): Make a **slip ring** *(see illustration)*, **ch 2** *(see Pattern Notes)*, 10 dc in ring, close ring, **join** *(see Pattern Notes)* in beg dc. *(10 dc)*

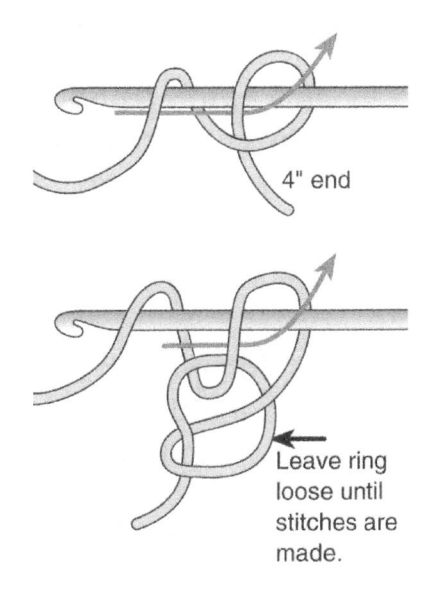

Slip Ring

Rnd 2: Ch 3 *(see Pattern Notes)*, dc in same st, 2 dc in each rem dc around, join in beg dc. *(20 dc)*

Rnd 3: Sl st into next dc, work **beg pc** *(see Special Stitches)* in same st, ch 3, sk next dc, [**pc** *(see Special Stitches)* in next dc, ch 3, sk next dc] around, join in beg pc. *(10 pc, 10 ch-3 sps)*

Rnd 4: Sl st into next ch-3 sp, **beg V-st** *(see Special Stitches)*, ch 2, [**V-st** *(see Special Stitches)* in next ch-3 sp, ch 2] around, join in 3rd ch of beg ch-3. *(10 V-sts, 10 ch-2 sps)*

Rnd 5: Sl st into next V-st ch sp, (ch 3, dc, ch 2, 2 dc, ch 1) all in same sp, (dc, ch 1) in next ch-2 sp, *(2 dc, ch 2, 2 dc, ch 1) in next V-st ch sp, (dc, ch 1) in next ch-2 sp, rep from * around, join in 3rd ch of beg ch-3. *(50 dc, 10 ch-2 sps, 20 ch-1 sps)*

Rnd 6: Sl st into next dc, ch 3, *(2 dc, ch 2, 2 dc) in next ch-2 sp, (dc, ch 1) in next dc, sk next dc, **fpdc** *(see Stitch Guide)* around next dc, ch 1**, sk next dc, dc in next dc, rep from * around, ending last rep at **, join in 3rd ch of beg ch-3. *(60 dc, 10 fpdc, 10 ch-2 sps, 20 ch-1 sps)*

Rnd 7: Sl st into next dc, ch 3, dc in next dc, *(2 dc, ch 2, 2 dc) in next ch-2 sp, dc in each of next 2 dc, ch 1, sk next dc, fpdc around next fpdc, ch 1, sk next dc**, dc in each of the next 2 dc, rep from * around, ending last rep at **, join in 3rd ch of beg ch-3. *(80 dc, 10 fpdc, 10 ch-2 sps, 20 ch-1 sps)*

Rnd 8: Sl st into next dc, ch 3, dc in each of the next 2 dc, *(2 dc, ch 2, 2 dc) in next ch-2 sp, dc in each of the next 3 dc, ch 1, sk next dc, fpdc around next fpdc, ch 1, sk next dc**, dc in each of the next 3 dc, rep from * around, ending last rep at **, join in 3rd ch of beg ch-3. *(100 dc, 10 fpdc, 10 ch-2 sps, 0 ch-1 sps)*

Rnd 9: Sl st into next dc, ch 1 loosely, **bpdc** *(see Stitch Guide)* around same dc and each dc across to ch-2 sp, *(2 dc, ch 2, 2 dc) in next ch-2 sp, bpdc around each dc until 1 dc before ch-1 sp, ch 1, sk next dc, fpdc around next fpdc, ch 1, sk next dc**, bpdc around each dc across to ch-2 sp, rep from * around, ending last rep at **, join in beg ch-1. *(40 dc, 80 bpdc, 10 fpdc, 10 ch-2 sps, 20 ch-1 sps)*

Rnds 10–12: Sl st into next dc, ch 3, *dc in each dc across to ch-2 sp, (2 dc, ch 2, 2 dc) in next ch-2 sp, dc in each dc until 1 dc before ch-1 sp, sk next dc, ch 1, fpdc around next fpdc, ch 1, sk next dc, rep from * around, join in 3rd ch of beg ch-3. *(180 dc, 10 fpdc, 10 ch-2 sps, 20 ch-1 sps)*

Rnds 13–40: [Rep rnds 9–12] 7 times. *(740 dc, 10 fpdc, 10 ch-2 sps, 20 ch-1 sps)*

Rnds 41–43: Rep rnds 9–11. *(800 dc, 10 fpdc, 10 ch-2 sps, 20 ch-1 sps)*

Rnd 44: Sl st in next dc, ch 3, dc in each of next 37 dc, *sk next dc, 5 dc in next ch-2 sp, sk next dc, dc in each of the next 38 dc, **dc dec** *(see Stitch Guide)* in next (dc, ch-1, fpdc, ch-1 and dc), sk next dc**, dc each of the next 38 dc, rep from * around, ending last rep at **, join in 3rd ch of beg ch-3. *(810 dc, 10 dec)*

Rnd 45: Reverse sc *(see Stitch Guide)* in each st around, fasten off.

SIX-POINTED STAR AFGHAN

An all-time favorite from the Annie's archive gets an update with on-trend colors for your modern home decor.

①②③④⑤⑥ **MODERATELY CHALLENGING**

FINISHED MEASUREMENT
69 inches in diameter

MATERIALS

- Premier Yarns Basix medium (worsted) weight acrylic yarn (7 oz/359 yds/200g per skein):
    3 skeins #1115-03 gray
    5 skeins #1115-04 black
    2 skeins #1115-02 light gray
    1 skein #1115-01 white
- Size I/9/5.5mm crochet hook or size needed to obtain gauge
- Tapestry needle

GAUGE
3 sc = 1 inch; 3 sc rows = 1 inch; 3 dc = 1 inch; 5 dc rows = 3 inches

SPECIAL STITCH
Double crochet decrease (dc dec): (Yo, insert hook, yo, draw lp through, draw through 2 lps on hook) in each of the sts indicated, yo, draw through all lps on hook.

AFGHAN

Rnd 1: With white, ch 6, dc in 6th ch from hook, [ch 2, dc in same ch] 4 times, ch 2, join with sl st in 3rd ch of beg ch-6. *(6 ch-2 sps)*

Rnd 2: Ch 3, (dc, ch 2, dc) in first ch-2 sp, *dc in next st, (dc, ch 2, dc) in next ch-2 sp; rep from * 4 times, join with sl st in top of beg ch-3. *(18 dc, 6 ch-2 sps)*

Rnd 3: Ch 3, dc in next st, *(2 dc, ch 2, dc) in next ch-2 sp, dc in each of next 3 sts; rep from * 4 times, (2 dc, ch 2, dc) in next ch-2 sp, dc in next st, join as before. Fasten off. *(36 dc, 6 ch-2 sps)*

Row 4: Now working in rows, join white with sl st in first dc after any ch-2 sp on rnd 3, ch 2, dc in each of next 5 sts, leaving remaining sts unworked, turn. *(6 dc)*

Row 5: Ch 2, dc in each of next 3 sts, **dc dec** *(see Special Stitch)* in next 2 sts, turn. *(5 sts)*

Row 6: Ch 2, dc in each of next 2 sts, dc dec in next 2 sts. *(4 sts)*

Row 7: Ch 2, dc dec in next 3 sts. Fasten off. [Rep rows 4–7 consecutively] 5 times. *(6 points)*

Rnd 8: Now working in rnds, join white with sl st in any ch-2 sp of rnd 3, ch 1, [sc in ch-2 sp, 8 sc up side of star spacing evenly, 3 sc at tip of point, 8 sc down side of point spacing evenly] around, join with sl st in first sc. Fasten off. *(120 sc)*

Note: *Work all rnds in back lps unless otherwise stated.*

Rnd 9: With back of star facing you, join light gray with sc in 115th st of rnd 8, sc in each of next 3 sts, [3 sc in next st, sc in each of next 8 sts, sk each of next 3 sts, sc in each of next 8 sts] 5 times, 3 sc in next st, sc in each of next 8 sts, sk each of next 3 sts, sc in each of last 4 sts, join as before, turn.

Rnd 10: Ch 1, sc in same st, sc in each of next 3 sts, [sk next 2 sts, sc in each of next 4 sts, 2 sc in next st, sc in each of next 3 sts, 3 sc in next st, sc in each of next 3 sts, 2 sc in next st, sc in each of next 4 sts] 5 times, sk next 2 sts, sc in each of next 4 sts, 2 sc in next st, sc in each of next 3 sts, 3 sc in next st, sc in each of next 3 sts, 2 sc in next st, join, turn. Fasten off.

Rnd 11: Join gray with sc in joining st of last rnd, sc in each of next 6 sts, 3 sc in next st, sc in each of next 9 sc, [sk next 2 sts, sc in each of next 9 sts, 3 sc in next st, sc in each of next 9 sts] 5 times, sk next 2 sts, sc in each of next 2 sts, join, turn.

Rnd 12: Ch 1, sc in each of first 2 sts, sk next 2 sts, sc in each of next 5 sts, 2 sc in next st, sc in each of next 3 sts, 3 sc in next st, [sc in each of next 3 sts, 2 sc in next st, sc in each of next 5 sts, sk next 2 sts, sc in each of next 5 sts, 2 sc in next st, sc in each of next 3 sts, 3 sc in next st] 5 times, sc in each of next 3 sts, 2 sc in next st, sc in each of next 3 sts, join, turn.

Rnd 13: Ch 1, sc in same st, sc in each of next 9 sts, [3 sc in next st, sc in each of next 10 sts, sk next 2 sts, sc in each of next 10 sts] 5 times, 3 sc in next st, sc in each of next 10 sts, sk next 2 sts, join, turn.

Rnd 14: Ch 1, sk first 2 sts, sc in each of next 5 sts, 2 sc in next st, sc in each of next 4 sts, 3 sc in next st, sc in each of next 4 sts, 2 sc in next st, sc in each of next 5 sts, [sk next 2 sts, sc in each of next 5 sts, 2 sc in next st, sc in each of next 4 sts, 3 sc in next st, sc in each of next 4 sts, 2 sc in next st, sc in each of next 5 sts] around, join, turn.

Rnd 15: Ch 1, sk next 2 sts, sc in each of next 11 sts, 3 sc in next st, [sc in each of next 11 sts, sk next 2 sts, sc in each of next 11 sts, 3 sc in next st] 5 times, sc in each of next 11 sts, join, turn. Fasten off.

Rnd 16: Sk first 7 sts, join black with sc in next st, sc in each of next 4 sts, 3 sc in next st, sc in each of next 5 sts, 2 sc in next st, sc in each of next 5 sts, sk next 2 sts, [sc in each of next 5 sts, 2 sc in next st, sc in each of next 5 sts, 3 sc in next st, sc in each of next 5 sts, 2 sc in next st, sc in each of next 5 sts, sk next 2 sts] 5 times, sc in each of next 5 sts, 2 sc in last st, join, turn.

Note: Outer point is the center st of 3-sc group.

Rnd 17: Skipping 2 sts at each inner point and working 3 sc in each outer point, ch 1, sc in each st around, turn.

Rnd 18: Ch 1, sc in first st, 2 sc in next st, sc in each of next 5 sts, [3 sc in next st, sc in each of next 5 sts, 2 sc in next st, sc in each of next 6 sts, sk next 2 sts, sc in each of next 6 sts, 2 sc in next st, sc in each of next 5 sts] 5 times, 3 sc in next st, sc in each of next 5 sts, 2 sc in next st, sc in each of next 6 sts, sk next 2 sts, sc in each of last 5 sts, join, turn.

Rnd 19: Rep rnd 17.

Rnd 20: Ch 1, sc in each of first 3 sts, 2 sc in next st, sc in each of next 6 sts, [3 sc in next st, sc in each of next 6 sts, 2 sc in next st, sc in each of next 6 sts, sk each of next 2 sts, sc in each of next 6 sts, 2 sc in next st, sc in each of next 6 sts] 5 times, 3 sc in next st, sc in each of next 6 sts, 2 sc in next st, sc in each of next 6 sts, sk next 2 sts, sc in each of last 3 sts, join, turn.

Rnd 21: Rep rnd 17. Fasten off.

Row 22: With front of star facing you, working in both lps, join white with sl st in 10th st from last outer point, ch 2, dc in each of next 3 sts, dc dec in next 4 sts, dc in each of next 2 sts, dc dec in next 2 sts, turn.

Row 23: Working in both lps, ch 2, dc dec in next 2 sts, dc in next st, dc dec in next 2 sts leaving last 2 sts unworked, turn.

Row 24: Ch 2, dc dec in next 3 sts. Fasten off.

Row 25: With front of star facing you, join white with sl st in same st as ch-2 of row 22, 8 sc evenly up side to point, 3 sc in tip of point, 8 sc evenly down side, sl st in same st as last dc of row 22. Fasten off.

Rep rows 22–25, joining in 10th st from each outer point around. After last point is made, turn. *(6 white points)*

Row 26: With back of star facing you, join light gray with sc in 6th st before any outer point of rnd 21, sc in next st, 2 sc in next st, sc in each of next 3 sts, [3 sc in next st, sc in each of next 3 sts, 2 sc in next st, sc in each of next 4 sts, sk next 2 sts, sc in each of next 4 sts, 2 sc in next st, sc in each of next 3 sts] 11 times, 3 sc in next st, sc in each of next 3 sts, 2 sc in next st, sc in each of next 4 sts, sk next 2 sts, sc in each of last 2 sts, join, turn.

Rnd 27: Rep rnd 17. Fasten off.

Rnd 28: Join gray with sc in 4th st from last outer point of last rnd, sc in each of next 3 sts, [3 sc in next st, sc in each of next 4 sts, 2 sc in next st, sc in each of next 4 sts, sk next 2 sts, sc in each of next 4 sts, 2 sc in next st, sc in each of next 4 sts] 11 times, 3 sc in next st, sc in each of next 4 sts, 2 sc in next st, sc in each of next 4 sts, sk next 2 sts, sc in each of next 4 sts, 2 sc in last st, join, turn.

Rnd 29: Rep rnd 17.

Rnd 30: Ch 1, sc in first st, 2 sc in next st, sc in each of next 4 sts, [3 sc in next st, sc in each of next 4 sts, 2 sc in next st, sc in each of next 5 sts, sk next 2 sts, sc in each of next 5 sts, 2 sc in next st, sc in each of next 4 sts] 11 times, 3 sc in next st, sc in each of next 4 sts, 2 sc in next st, sc in each of next 5 sts, sk next 2 sts, sc in each of last 4 sts, join, turn.

Rnd 31: Rep rnd 17. Fasten off.

Rnd 32: Join black with sc in 5th st from last outer point, sc in each of next 4 sts, [3 sc in next st, sc in each of next 5 sts, 2 sc in next st, sc in each of next 5 sts, sk next 2 sts, sc in each of next 5 sts, 2 sc in next st, sc in each of next 5 sts] 11 times, 3 sc in next st, sc in each of next 5 sts, 2 sc in next st, sc in each of next 5 sts, sk next 2 sts, sc in each of next 5 sts, 2 sc in last st, join, turn.

Rnd 33: Rep rnd 17.

Rnd 34: Rep rnd 18, working instructions between [ ] 11 times.

Rnd 35: Rep rnd 17.

Rnd 36: Rep rnd 20, working instructions between [ ] 11 times.

Rnd 37: Rep rnd 17. Fasten off.

Rnd 38: Join light gray with sc in 6th st from outer point, sc in each of next 5 sts, *[3 sc in next st, sc in each of next 6 sts, 2 sc in next st, sc in each of next 7 sts, sk next 2 sts, sc in each of next 7 sts, 2 sc in next st, sc in each of next 6 sts] 11 times, 3 sc in next st, sc in each of next 6 sts, 2 sc in next st, sc in each of next 7 sts, sk next 2 sts, sc in each of next 7 sts, 2 sc in last st, join, turn.

Rnd 39: Rep rnd 17. Fasten off.

Rnd 40: Join gray with sc in 6th st from outer point, sc in each of next 5 sts, *[3 sc in next st, sc in each of next 6 sts, 2 sc in next st, sc in each of next 8 sts, sk next 2 sts, sc in each of next 8 sts, 2 sc in next st, sc in each of next 6 sts] 11 times, 3 sc in next st, sc in each of next 6 sts, 2 sc in next st, sc in each of next 8 sts, sk each of next 2 sts, sc in each of next 8 sts, 2 sc in last st, join, turn.

Rnd 41: Rep rnd 17.

Rnd 42: Ch 1, 2 sc in first st, *sc in each of next 7 sts, [3 sc in next st, sc in each of next 7 sts, 2 sc in next st, sc in each of next 8 sts, sk next 2 sts, sc in each of next 8 sts, 2 sc in next st, sc in each of next 7 sts] 11 times, 3 sc in next st, sc in each of next 7 sts, 2 sc in next st, sc in each of next 8 sts, sk next 2 sts, sc in each of last 8 sts, join, turn.

Rnd 43: Rep rnd 17. Fasten off.

Rnd 44: Join black with sc in 8th st from outer point, sc in each of next 7 sts, [3 sc in next st, sc in each of next 8 sts, 2 sc in next st, sc in each of next 8 sts, sk next 2 sts, sc in each of next 8 sts, 2 sc in next st, sc in each of next 8 sts] 11 times, 3 sc in next st, sc in each of next 8 sts, 2 sc in next st, sc in each of next 8 sts, sk next 2 sts, sc in each of next 8 sts, 2 sc in last st, join, turn.

Rnd 45: Rep rnd 17.

Rnd 46: Ch 1, sc in first st, 2 sc in next st, sc in each of next 8 sts, [3 sc in next st, sc in each of next 8 sts, 2 sc in next st, sc in each of next 9 sts, sk next 2 sts, sc in each of next 9 sts, 2 sc in next st, sc in each of next 8 sts] 11 times, 3 sc in next st, sc in each of next 8 sts, 2 sc in next st, sc in each of next 9 sts, sk next 2 sts, sc in each of next 8 sts, join, turn.

Rnd 47: Rep rnd 17.

Rnd 48: Ch 1, sc in each of first 3 sts, 2 sc in next st, sc in each of next 9 sts, [3 sc in next st, sc in each of next 9 sts, 2 sc in next st, sc in each of next 9 sts, sk next 2 sts, sc in each of next 9 sts, 2 sc in next st, sc in each of next 9 sts] 11 times, 3 sc in next st, sc in each of next 9 sts, 2 sc in next st, sc in each of next 9 sts, sk next 2 sts, sc in each of last 6 sts, join, turn.

Rnd 49: Rep rnd 17. Fasten off.

Row 50: With front of star facing you, working in both lps, join white with sl st in 12th st from outer point, ch 2, dc in each of next 7 sts, dc dec in next 4 sts, dc in each of next 6 sts, dc dec in next 2 sts, turn.

Row 51: Working in both lps, ch 2, dc in each of next 4 sts, (dc dec in next 2 sts) twice, dc in each of next 4 sts, dc dec in next 2 sts leaving last st unworked, turn.

Row 52: Ch 2, dc in each of next 3 sts, (dc dec in next 2 sts) twice, dc in next st, dc dec in next 2 sts leaving last st unworked, turn.

Row 53: Ch 2, dc in next st, dc dec in next 3 sts, dc in each of next 2 sts leaving last st unworked, turn.

Row 54: Ch 2, [sk next st, dc in next st leaving last 2 lps on hook] twice, yo, draw through all lps on hook. Fasten off.

Row 55: With front of star facing you, join white with sl st in same st as ch 2 of row 50, 10 sc evenly up side to point, 3 sc in tip of point, 10 sc evenly down side, sl st in same st as last dc of row 50. Fasten off.

Rep rows 50–55, joining in 12th st of each outer point. *(12 points)*

Rnd 56: With back of star facing you, join light gray with sc in 6th st before any outer point of rnd 49, 2 sc in next st, sc in each of next 4 sts, [3 sc in next st, sc in each of next 4 sts, 2 sc in next st, sc in each of next 5 sts, sk next 2 sts, sc in each of next 5 sts, 2 sc in next st, sc in each of next 4 sts] 23 times, 3 sc in next st, sc in each of next 4 sts, 2 sc in next st, sc in each of next 5 sts, sk next 2 sts, sc in each of last 4 sts, join, turn.

Rnd 57: Rep rnd 17. Fasten off.

Rnd 58: Joining gray, rep rnd 32, working instructions between [ ] 23 times.

Rnd 59: Rep rnd 17.

Rnd 60: Rep rnd 18, working instructions between [ ] 23 times.

Rnd 61: Rep rnd 17. Fasten off.

Rnd 62: Join black with sc in 4th st from outer point, sc in each of next 3 sts, [3 sc in next st, sc in each of next 6 sts, 2 sc in next st, sc in each of next 6 sts, sk next 2 sts, sc in each of next 6 sts, 2 sc in next st, sc in each of next 6 sts] 23 times, 3 sc in next st, sc in each of next 6 sts, 2 sc in next st, sc in each of next 6 sts, sk next 2 sts, sc in each of next 6 sts, 2 sc in next st, sc in each of last 2 sts, join, turn.

Rnd 63: Rep rnd 17.

Rnd 64: Ch 1, sc in each of first 6 sts, rep from * in rnd 38, working between [ ] 23 times.

Rnd 65: Rep rnd 17.

Rnd 66: Ch 1, sc in first st, 2 sc in next st, sc in each of next 6 sts, [3 sc in next st, sc in each of next 6 sts, 2 sc in next st, sc in each of next 8 sts, sk next 2 sts, sc in each of next 8 sts, 2 sc in next st, sc in each of next 6 sts] 23 times, 3 sc in next st, sc in each of next 6 sts, 2 sc in next st, sc in each of next 8 sts, sk next 2 sts, sc in each of next 7 sts, join, turn.

Rnd 67: Rep rnd 17. Fasten off.

Rnd 68: Join light gray in 8th st from outer point with (sl st, ch 1, 2 sc) in same st; rep from * in rnd 42, working between [ ] 23 times.

Rnd 69: Rep rnd 17. Fasten off.

Rnd 70: Joining gray, rep rnd 44, working between [ ] 23 times.

Rnd 71: Rep rnd 17.

Rnd 72: Rep rnd 46, working between [ ] 23 times.

Rnd 73: Rep rnd 17. Fasten off.

Rnd 74: Joining black with sl st in 13th st from outer point, rep rnd 48, working between [ ] 23 times.

Rnd 75: Rep rnd 17.

Rnd 76: Ch 1, sc in first 6 sts, 2 sc in next st, sc in each of next 9 sts, [3 sc in next st, sc in each of next 9 sts, 2 sc in next st, sc in each of next 10 sts, sk next 2 sts, sc in each of next 10 sts, 2 sc in next st, sc in each of next 9 sts] 23 times, 3 sc in next st, sc in each of next 9 sts, 2 sc in next st, sc in each of next 10 sts, sk next 2 sts, sc in each of last 4 sts, join, turn.

Rnd 77: Rep rnd 17.

Rnd 78: Ch 1, sc in each of first 8 sts, 2 sc in next st, sc in each of next 10 sts, [3 sc in next st, sc in each of next 10 sts, 2 sc in next st, sc in each of next 10 sts, sk next 2 sts, sc in each of next 10 sts, 2 sc in next st, sc in each of next 10 sts] 23 times, 3 sc in next st, sc in each of next 10 sts, 2 sc in next st, sc in each of next 10 sts, sk next 2 sts, sc in each of last 2 sts, join, turn.

Rnd 79: Rep rnd 17.

Rnd 80: Ch 1, sc in each of first 11 sts, 2 sc in next st, sc in each of next 10 sts, [3 sc in next st, sc in each of next 10 sts, 2 sc in next st, sc in each of next 11 sts, sk next 2 sts, sc in each of next 11 sts, 2 sc in next st, sc in each of next 10 sts] 23 times, 3 sc in next st, sc in each of next 10 sts, 2 sc in next st, sc in each of next 11 sts, sk last 2 sts, join. Fasten off.

ROUNDABOUT THROW

Shades of saturated colors are crocheted in rounds of textural stitches from the center out, creating a stunning color burst effect.

①②③④⑤⑥ **EASY**

FINISHED MEASUREMENT
52 inches in diameter

MATERIALS

- Red Heart Soft medium (worsted) weight acrylic yarn (5 oz/256 yds/141g per ball):
    2 balls each #3729 grape, #4608 wine, #4360 cocoa, #9263 cinnabar and #9274 biscuit
- Size I/9/5.5mm crochet hook or size needed to obtain gauge
- Tapestry needle

GAUGE
Rnds 1–4 = 5 inches in diameter

PATTERN NOTES
Weave in loose ends as work progresses.

Join with slip stitch as indicated unless otherwise stated.

Chain-3 at beginning of round counts as first double crochet unless otherwise stated. When instructed to work in a V-stitch, work in space between 2 double crochet.

SPECIAL STITCHES
Beginning V-stitch (beg V-st): Ch 3, dc in indicated st.
V-stitch (V-st): 2 dc in indicated st.
Beginning side shell (beg side shell): (**Sc join**—*see Special Stitches*, ch 2, 2 dc) in indicated sp.
Single crochet join (sc join): Place a slip knot on hook, insert hook in indicated st, yo and pull up a lp, yo and draw through both lps on hook.
Side shell: (Sc, ch 2, 2 dc) in indicated sp.
Shell: 3 dc in indicated st or sp.
Fan: 5 dc in indicated st.

THROW
Rnd 1: With wine, ch 4, 11 dc in 4th ch from hook *(beg sk chs count as first dc)*, **join** *(see Pattern Notes)* in top of beg ch-3. *(12 dc)*

Rnd 2: **Beg V-st** *(see Special Stitches)* in same st as join, **V-st** *(see Special Stitches)* in each st around, join in top of beg ch-3, fasten off. *(12 V-sts)*

Rnd 3: With cinnabar, work **beg side shell** *(see Special Stitches)* in sp between any 2 V-sts, *sk next V-st**, **side shell** *(see Special Stitches)* in next sp, rep from * around, ending last rep at **, join in beg sc, fasten off. *(12 side shells)*

Rnd 4: Sc join grape in ch-2 sp of any side shell, *sk next 2 dc, **shell** *(see Special Stitches)* in next sc**, sc in next ch-2 sp, rep from * around, ending last rep at **, join in beg sc, fasten off. *(12 shells, 12 sc)*

Rnd 5: Sc join biscuit in 2nd dc of any shell, *sk next dc, shell in next sc, sk next dc**, sc in next dc, rep from * around, ending last rep at **, join in beg sc. *(12 shells, 12 sc)*

Rnd 6: Beg V-st in same st as join, *sk next dc, V-st in next dc, sk next dc**, V-st in next sc, rep from * around, ending last rep at **, join, fasten off. *(24 V-sts)*

Rnd 7: With cocoa, work beg side shell between any 2 V-sts, *sk next V-st**, side shell in next sp, rep from * around, ending last rep at **, join in beg sc, fasten off. *(24 side shells)*

Rnd 8: Sc join wine in ch-2 sp of any side shell, *sk next 2 dc, V-st in next sc**, sc in next ch-2 sp, rep from * around, ending last rep at **, join in beg sc. *(24 V-sts, 24 sc)*

Rnd 9: Ch 1, sc in same st as join, *shell **in next V-st** *(see Pattern Notes)***, sc in next sc, rep from * around, ending last rep at **, join in beg sc, fasten off. *(24 shells, 24 sc)*

Rnd 10: With cinnabar, rep rnd 5. *(24 shells, 24 sc)*

Rnd 11: Sl st in next dc, ch 3, dc in each of next 2 dc, *sk next sc, dc in each of next 3 dc, rep from * around, join in top of beg ch-3, fasten off. *(72 dc)*

Rnd 12: With grape, work beg side shell in sp between any 2 dc, *sk next 2 dc**, side shell in sp between previous and next dc, rep from * around, ending last rep at **, join in sc of beg side shell, fasten off. *(36 side shells)*

Rnds 13 & 14: With biscuit, rep rnds 8 and 9. *(36 shells, 36 sc)*

Rnds 15 & 16: With cocoa, rep rnds 10 and 11. *(108 dc)*

Rnd 17: With wine, rep rnd 12. *(54 side shells)*

Rnds 18 & 19: With cinnabar, rep rnds 8 and 9. *(54 shells, 54 sc)*

Rnd 20: Sc join grape in 2nd dc of any shell, *sk next dc, V-st in next sc, sk next dc**, sc in next dc, rep from * around, ending last rep at **, join in beg sc. *(54 V-sts, 54 sc)*

Rnd 21: With grape, rep rnd 9. *(54 shells, 54 sc)*

Rnds 22 & 23: With biscuit, rep rnds 10 and 11. *(162 dc)*

Rnd 24: With cocoa, work beg side shell in any sp between 3-dc groups, *sk next 3 dc, (side shell in next sp, sk next 2 dc) 3 times**, side shell in next sp, rep from * around, ending last rep at **, join in beg sc, fasten off. *(72 side shells)*

Rnds 25 & 26: With wine, rep rnds 8 and 9. *(72 shells, 72 sc)*

Rnds 27 & 28: With cinnabar, rep rnds 20 and 21.

Rnds 29 & 30: With grape, rep rnds 20 and 21.

Rnds 31 & 32: With biscuit, rep rnds 20 and 21.

Rnds 33 & 34: With cocoa, rep rnds 10 and 11. *(216 dc)*

Rnd 35: With wine, rep rnd 24. *(96 side shells)*

Rnds 36 & 37: With cinnabar, rep rnds 8 and 9. *(96 shells, 96 sc)*

Rnds 38 & 39: With grape, rep rnds 20 and 21.

Rnds 40 & 41: With biscuit, rep rnds 20 and 21.

Rnds 42 & 43: With cocoa, rep rnds 20 and 21.

Rnds 44 & 45: With wine, rep rnds 10 and 11. *(288 dc)*

Rnd 46: With cinnabar, rep rnd 24. *(128 side shells)*

Rnds 47 & 48: With grape, rep rnds 8 and 9.

Rnds 49 & 50: With biscuit, rep rnds 20 and 21.

Rnds 51 & 52: With cocoa, rep rnds 20 and 21.

Rnds 53 & 54: With wine, rep rnds 20 and 21.

Rnds 55 & 56: With cinnabar, rep rnds 20 and 21.

Rnds 57 & 58: With grape, rep rnds 20 and 21.

Rnds 59 & 60: With biscuit, rep rnds 20 and 21.

Rnd 61: With cocoa, rep rnd 5.

Rnd 62: With wine, rep rnd 5.

Rnd 63: Ch 1, sl st in next dc, sc in next dc, *sk next dc**, **fan** *(see Special Stitches)* in next sc, sk next dc, sc in next dc, rep from * around, ending last rep at **, fan in same sl st as join, join in beg sc, fasten off.

STITCH GUIDE

Need help? ▶ **StitchGuide.com** • ILLUSTRATED GUIDES • HOW-TO VIDEOS

STITCH ABBREVIATIONS

beg	begin/begins/beginning
bpdc	back post double crochet
bpsc	back post single crochet
bptr	back post treble crochet
CC	contrasting color
ch(s)	chain(s)
ch-	refers to chain or space previously made (i.e., ch-1 space)
ch sp(s)	chain space(s)
cl(s)	cluster(s)
cm	centimeter(s)
dc	double crochet (singular/plural)
dc dec	double crochet 2 or more stitches together, as indicated
dec	decrease/decreases/decreasing
dtr	double treble crochet
ext	extended
fpdc	front post double crochet
fpsc	front post single crochet
fptr	front post treble crochet
g	gram(s)
hdc	half double crochet
hdc dec	half double crochet 2 or more stitches together, as indicated
inc	increase/increases/increasing
lp(s)	loop(s)
MC	main color
mm	millimeter(s)
oz	ounce(s)
pc	popcorn(s)

rem	remain/remains/remaining
rep(s)	repeat(s)
rnd(s)	round(s)
RS	right side
sc	single crochet (singular/plural)
sc dec	single crochet 2 or more stitches together, as indicated
sk	skip/skipped/skipping
sl st(s)	slip stitch(es)
sp(s)	space(s)/spaced
st(s)	stitch(es)
tog	together
tr	treble crochet
trtr	triple treble
WS	wrong side
yd(s)	yard(s)
yo	yarn over

YARN CONVERSION

OUNCES TO GRAMS	GRAMS TO OUNCES
1 .... 28.4	25 .... 7/8
2 .... 56.7	40 .... 1 2/3
3 .... 85.0	50 .... 1 3/4
4 .... 113.4	100 .... 3 1/2

UNITED STATES		UNITED KINGDOM
sl st (slip stitch)	=	sc (single crochet)
sc (single crochet)	=	dc (double crochet)
hdc (half double crochet)	=	htr (half treble crochet)
dc (double crochet)	=	tr (treble crochet)
tr (treble crochet)	=	dtr (double treble crochet)
dtr (double treble crochet)	=	ttr (triple treble crochet)
skip	=	miss

Single crochet decrease (sc dec): (Insert hook, yo, draw lp through) in each of the sts indicated, yo, draw through all lps on hook.

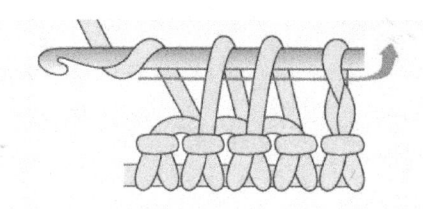

Example of 2-sc dec

Half double crochet decrease (hdc dec): (Yo, insert hook, yo, draw lp through) in each of the sts indicated, yo, draw through all lps on hook.

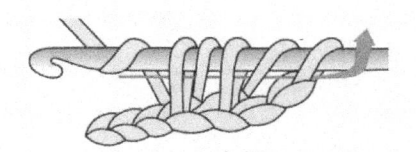

Example of 2-hdc dec

Reverse single crochet (reverse sc): Ch 1, sk first st, working from left to right, insert hook in next st from front to back, draw up lp on hook, yo and draw through both lps on hook.

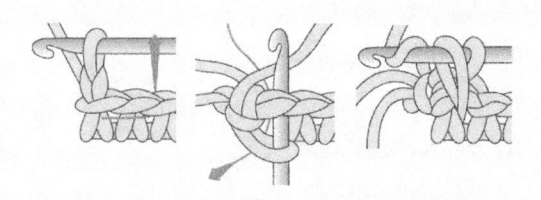

Chain (ch): Yo, pull through lp on hook.

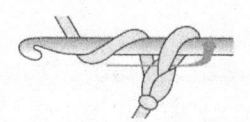

Single crochet (sc): Insert hook in st, yo, pull through st, yo, pull through both lps on hook.

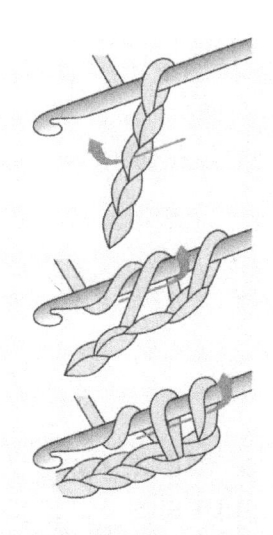

Double crochet (dc): Yo, insert hook in st, yo, pull through st, [yo, pull through 2 lps] twice.

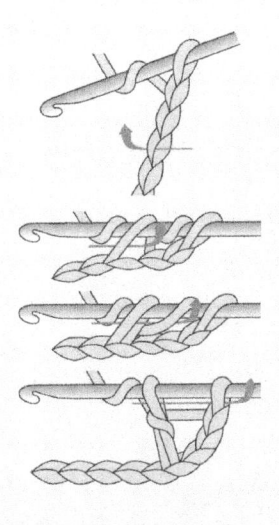

Double crochet decrease (dc dec): (Yo, insert hook, yo, draw lp through, yo, draw through 2 lps on hook) in each of the sts indicated, yo, draw through all lps on hook.

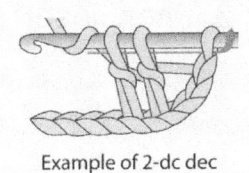

Example of 2-dc dec

Front loop (front lp) Back loop (back lp)

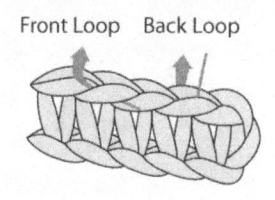

Front post stitch (fp): Back post stitch (bp): When working post st, insert hook from right to left around post of st on previous row.

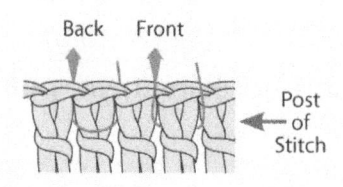

Half double crochet (hdc): Yo, insert hook in st, yo, pull through st, yo, pull through all 3 lps on hook.

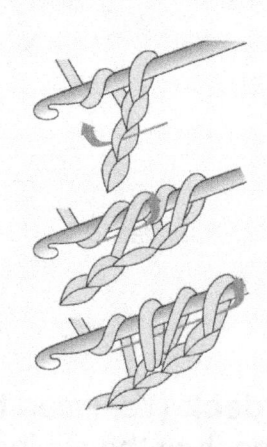

Double treble crochet (dtr): Yo 3 times, insert hook in st, yo, pull through st, [yo, pull through 2 lps] 4 times.

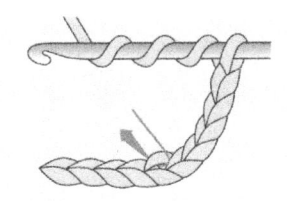

Treble crochet decrease (tr dec): Holding back last lp of each st, tr in each of the sts indicated, yo, pull through all lps on hook.

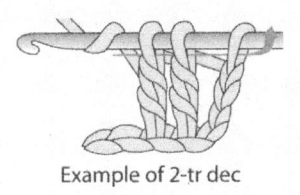

Example of 2-tr dec

Slip stitch (sl st): Insert hook in st, pull through both lps on hook.

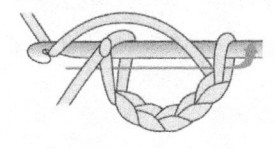

Chain color change (ch color change) Yo with new color, draw through last lp on hook.

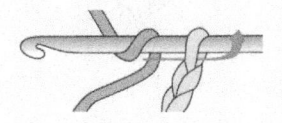

Double crochet color change (dc color change) Drop first color, yo with new color, draw through last 2 lps of st.

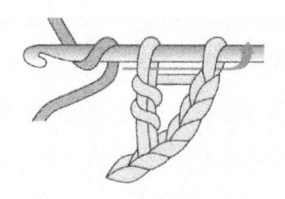

Treble crochet (tr): Yo twice, insert hook in st, yo, pull through st, [yo, pull through 2 lps] 3 times.

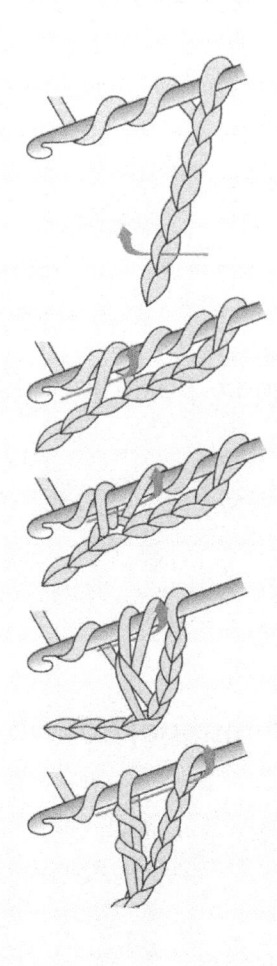

METRIC CONVERSION CHARTS

METRIC CONVERSIONS

yards	x	.9144	=	meters (m)
yards	x	91.44	=	centimeters (cm)
inches	x	2.54	=	centimeters (cm)
inches	x	25.40	=	millimeters (mm)
inches	x	.0254	=	meters (m)

centimeters	x	.3937	=	inches
meters	x	1.0936	=	yards

INCHES INTO MILLIMETERS & CENTIMETERS (Rounded off slightly)

inches	mm	cm	inches	cm	inches	cm	inches	cm
1/8	3	0.3	5	12.5	21	53.5	38	96.5
1/4	6	0.6	5 1/2	14	22	56	39	99
3/8	10	1	6	15	23	58.5	40	101.5
1/2	13	1.3	7	18	24	61	41	104
5/8	15	1.5	8	20.5	25	63.5	42	106.5
3/4	20	2	9	23	26	66	43	109
7/8	22	2.2	10	25.5	27	68.5	44	112
1	25	2.5	11	28	28	71	45	114.5
1 1/4	32	3.2	12	30.5	29	73.5	46	117
1 1/2	38	3.8	13	33	30	76	47	119.5
1 3/4	45	4.5	14	35.5	31	79	48	122
2	50	5	15	38	32	81.5	49	124.5
2 1/2	65	6.5	16	40.5	33	84	50	127
3	75	7.5	17	43	34	86.5		
3 1/2	90	9	18	46	35	89		
4	100	10	19	48.5	36	91.5		
4 1/2	115	11.5	20	51	37	94		

KNITTING NEEDLES CONVERSION CHART

Canada/U.S.	0	1	2	3	4	5	6	7	8	9	10	10½	11	13	15
Metric (mm)	2	2¼	2¾	3¼	3½	3¾	4	4½	5	5½	6	6½	8	9	10

CROCHET HOOKS CONVERSION CHART

Canada/U.S.	1/B	2/C	3/D	4/E	5/F	6/G	7	8/H	9/I	10/J	10½/K	N
Metric (mm)	2.25	2.75	3.25	3.5	3.75	4	4.5	5	5.5	6	6.5	9.0

142